"Kosher and Halal certification is becoming increasingly important in both food industry and other types of companies. But even though it can be difficult to navigate in this blend of religion, science and business, no actual guidebook has existed until now. 'Kosher and Halal Business Compliance' fills this gap and gives a good introduction to this fascinating world."

– Jes Knudsen, Global Kosher/Halal coordinator,
Novozymes, Denmark

"At last, a text that simply explains how to achieve a religious standard without the mystery and magic that often surrounds these things. Like anyone in the food industry, I am keen for ideas on how to meet customer standards and promote understanding with all concerned."

– Steven Maloney, Kitchen Range Foods

Kosher and Halal Business Compliance

Kosher is a Hebrew term meaning 'fit' or 'proper', and halal is an Arabic word that literally means 'permissible' or 'lawful'. Within the last two decades or so, kosher and halal markets have become global in scope, and states, manufacturers, restaurants, shops, certifiers and consumers around the world are faced with ever stricter and more complex requirements – most clearly exemplified by Muslim and Jewish groups' call for kosher and halal certification by third-party certification bodies. During this period, hundreds of kosher and halal certifiers have emerged around the world, and while thousands of manufacturers, restaurants and shops have been certified, the majority have not.

Kosher and halal requirements are comparable, but there are also many differences, and the book discusses how these similarities and differences affect production, trade and regulation around the world. The authors' research demonstrates that there is a need to address kosher and halal markets simultaneously and answers the question '*what characterizes global kosher and halal markets, and how can businesses comply with the rising demands and requirements that have emerged?*'

This is the only book of its kind and it will appeal to manufacturing companies, restaurants and shops that already are or want to be kosher/halal certified. The book can also be assigned in a variety of upper-level undergraduate courses and graduate seminars in business studies, management and marketing. Moreover, the book will be of interest to readers in the natural sciences (for example, food scientists) and to state as well as non-state kosher/halal certification bodies, policy makers, interest groups and consultants. *Kosher and Halal Business Compliance* is accessible in style, global in scope and based on decades of research.

John Lever is Senior Lecturer at the University of Huddersfield Business School. His work on the food industry focusses on kosher and halal meat markets, farm animal welfare and food sustainability. He also conducts consultancy in the international halal market.

Johan Fischer is Associate Professor in the Department of Social Sciences and Business, Roskilde University, Denmark. His work focuses on modern religion and markets in global perspective. More specifically, Johan explores the interfaces between class, consumption, market relations, religion and the state in a globalised world.

Kosher and Halal Business Compliance

John Lever and Johan Fischer

Routledge
Taylor & Francis Group

LONDON AND NEW YORK

First published 2019
by Routledge
2 Park Square, Milton Park, Abingdon, Oxon OX14 4RN

and by Routledge
711 Third Avenue, New York, NY 10017

Routledge is an imprint of the Taylor & Francis Group, an informa business

© 2019 John Lever and Johan Fischer

The right of Johan Fischer and John Lever to be identified as
authors of this work has been asserted by them in accordance with
sections 77 and 78 of the Copyright, Designs and Patents Act 1988.

British Library Cataloguing-in-Publication Data
A catalogue record for this book is available from the British Library

Library of Congress Cataloging-in-Publication Data
A catalog record for this book has been requested

ISBN: 978-1-13806-518-5 (hbk)
ISBN: 978-1-31515-987-4 (ebk)

Typeset in Bembo
by Apex CoVantage, LLC

Contents

Jewish and Arabic terms

Dhabh	Islamic ritual slaughter
glatt	a Yiddish word meaning 'smooth'
Halacha	Jewish law
haram	unlawful/forbidden
Kashrut	Jewish dietary laws
Rabbi	a scholar of Jewish law
Shechita	Jewish ritual slaughter
Sunnah	the life, actions and teachings of the Prophet Muhammad
treifa	unfit/non kosher
ulama	Islamic scholars

Part I
Overview

1 Introduction

Kosher is a Hebrew term meaning 'fit' or 'proper'. Halal is an Arabic word that literally means 'permissible' or 'lawful'. This introductory chapter explains why and how kosher and halal markets have expanded globally during the last couple of decades. We review sources relevant to business organisations and demonstrate how our book fills a gap in the market. We show how the book is organised into chapters that each in their own way explain what the central challenges are for business and how these challenges can be overcome.

Kosher and halal products (particularly meat) can be traced back thousands of years, but within the last two decades in particular the markets for kosher and halal food and other products have grown rapidly to become global in scope. During this period, states, manufacturers, restaurants, shops, certifiers and consumers have been presented with stricter and more complex kosher and halal requirements in line with the growth of third-party certification bodies that have emerged to assure consumer confidence in this rapidly changing context. Hundreds of kosher and halal certifiers have emerged in many countries around the world, and thousands of manufacturers, restaurants, shops and products have been certified.

The kosher market first began to expand in the middle decades of the 20th century, and today kosher consumption is growing steadily among religious and also non-religious consumers. In the US, more than 60% of all kosher food consumption is now linked to non-religious values associated with health and food quality; many Muslim consumers also accept kosher products, notably when halal availability is limited. Globally there are estimated to be around 25 million kosher consumers, and in 2008 sales of kosher foods in the US totalled $12.5 billion (Mintel 2009). Kosher is one of the oldest food assurance systems in the world and despite the widespread acceptance of common practices there are many independent kosher certification bodies. The Orthodox Union (OU) is perhaps the best-known global kosher certification body among the Big Five kosher certification bodies in the US (see Chapter 6), but there are many other national, regional and local rabbinical authorities and Jewish courts of law offering *kashrut* (Jewish religious dietary laws) services.

The market for halal products has also grown rapidly in recent decades and the value of the halal food market alone has been estimated at around $632 billion annually (Bergeaud-Blackler, Lever and Fischer 2015). The Muslim population is projected to increase globally from 1.6 billion to 2.2 billion by 2030 and the potential for market growth has been widely recognised. In the coming decades, the halal market is expected to grow by more than 100% in some locations and the demand for certified halal meat products is predicted to expand rapidly (Miller 2009). In recent decades, Southeast Asian countries such as Indonesia, Malaysia, Singapore, Brunei and Thailand developed the first halal standards and certification systems for internal and latterly for external markets (Fischer 2011, 2015a). Today, new players from the United Arab Emirates (UAE) and other Middle Eastern countries are entering the market.

Although kosher and halal requirements are different in some ways, they are comparable in others, and many companies indicate that halal certification is more easily acquired if the company is already kosher certified. Quite a number of non-meat products can be certified as both kosher and halal, products such as falafel, for example, and our research demonstrates that there is a need to address kosher and halal markets simultaneously (Fischer 2015a; Lever and Fischer 2018). Global in scope and based on decades of empirically grounded research, this book explores what the main challenges are for businesses working in or thinking about entering these markets and how these challenges can be addressed. The research question answered in the book is this: *What characterizes global kosher and halal markets, and how can business comply with the rising demands and requirements that have emerged?*

During long periods of research and consultancy, we found that state agencies, manufacturers, shops and restaurants would like to have a book that explains modern and global kosher and halal. To our knowledge, there is no competing book in English on the market. The book is aimed at manufacturing companies, restaurants and shops that already are or want to be kosher and/or halal certified. It will also be useful for a variety of upper-level undergraduate courses and graduate seminars in business studies, management and marketing. It will also be of interest to readers in the natural sciences (for example, food scientists) and similarly outside academia for state as well as for non-state kosher and halal certification bodies, policy makers and consultants.

There is a body of literature on kosher and halal in food production, which is typically written by Jewish and Muslim food scientists, including, most notably, *Kosher Food Production* (Blech 2008) and *Halal Food Production* (Riaz and Chaudry 2004). Joe Regenstein of Cornell University's Department of Food Science has written extensively on kosher but also on halal from a food science perspective. The present book is also based on research in our book for the academic market: *Religion, Regulation, Consumption: Globalising Kosher and Halal Markets* (Lever and Fischer 2018). These sources are somewhat 'academic' and technical in their discussion of kosher and halal, and they do not offer systematic comparisons between the two. This book is different in that it has a comparative perspective. Based on our extensive research among certifiers and companies, we explain how businesses understand and practice kosher and halal and how other organisations can learn from these findings.

Organisation of the book

After this introduction, Part I continues with Chapter 2, which explains the underlying principles of kosher and halal, and Chapter 3, which explores their similarities and differences. In Part II of the book, Chapter 4 focuses on certification, inspections and logos, and we discuss how businesses can address challenges related to religious inspections and the design/placement of kosher/halal logos. Chapter 5 examines kosher/halal standards as 'formal' standards and also as 'practical standards' used in production. Chapter 6 lists and discusses important types of kosher and halal certifiers and the experiences of businesses working with these certifiers, while Chapter 7 briefly explores the role of government in kosher and halal production and trade. Chapter 8 reviews research on kosher and halal consumption in the everyday lives of Muslims and Jews in different geographical contexts, offering a general fourfold categorisation of consumers. Chapter 9 starts off Part III with a focus on meat production, the primary historical market for kosher and halal. Chapter 10 then deals with biotech, Chapter 11 with dairy production, 12 with bread and bakery, before Chapter 13 looks at fruit and vegetables. In Chapter 14 and 15 we turn to shops and restaurants respectively, before Chapter 16 examines the food service industry in public institutions. This is followed by Chapter 17, which examines how religious principles are shaping new knowledge, work processes and certification practices. Chapter 18 looks at developments in 'religious science', before Chapter 19 ties the findings of the book together and reflects on the challenges and opportunities kosher and halal present for business organisations.

Bibliography

Bergeaud-Blackler, F., Lever, J. and Fischer, J. (eds) (2015) *Halal Matters: Islam, Politics, and Markets in Global Perspective*. New York: Routledge.

Blech, Z.Y. (2008) *Kosher Food Production*. Ames, IA: Wiley-Blackwell.

Fischer, J. (2011) *The Halal Frontier: Muslim Consumers in a Globalized Market*. New York: Palgrave Macmillan.

Fischer, J. (2015a) *Islam, Standards and Technoscience: In Global Halal Zones*. London and New York: Routledge.

Fischer, J. (2015b) Keeping enzymes kosher: Sacred and secular biotech production. EMBO Reports.

Lever, J. and Fischer, J. (2018) *Religion, Regulation, Consumption: Globalising Kosher and Halal Markets*. Manchester: Manchester University Press.

Miller, T. (2009) Mapping the Global Muslim Population, A Report on the Size and Distribution of the World's Muslim Population, Pew Research Centre.

Mintel (2009) *Kosher Foods – US –* January 2009.

Riaz, M. N. and Chaudry, M. M. (2004) *Halal Food Production*. Boca Raton, FL: CRC Press.

2 What is kosher and halal?

Kashrut and kosher law (*halacha*) date back several thousand years. As a system of regulation and food assurance it is based on a number of verses found in religious texts and the decisions of rabbinic authorities, as originally outlined in the Torah, the first five 'Books of Moses' (specifically Exodus, Leviticus and Deuteronomy) and texts linked to the Talmud. These include:

- 'Any animal that has true hoofs, with clefts through the hoofs, and that chews the cud–such you may eat . . . And the swine – although it has true hoofs, with the hoofs cleft through, it does not chew the cud: it is impure for you' (Leviticus 11:3, 11:7);
- 'Thou shalt not seethe a kid in its mother's milk' (Exod. XXXIV, 26; Duet XIV, 21) and;
- 'You shall not kill of thy heard and thy flock which the Lord hath given you, except as I have commanded you' (Duet 12:21).

Meat only qualifies as kosher if the animal of origin is slaughtered using appropriate methods (*shechita*) as interpreted through these commentaries and traditional customs and practice. As well as the proscribed method of slaughter, there are a number of other prohibitions such as a ban on pork, the mixing of milk and meat and the acceptability/unacceptability of specific species of animals and plants. Jews are only permitted to consume the meat of animals that 'chew the cud' and have 'cloven hooves', for example, cattle, sheep and goats; sea creatures with fins and scales are acceptable, whereas shellfish are not.

Other important concerns relate to rennin, gelatine, lactose, sodium caseinate (a protein produced from casein in skimmed milk), vitamins, eggs, grape products, fruits, vegetables and Passover (a major Jewish festival) items, which we will deal with in relevant chapters. In sum, kosher law is the application of a system of religious precepts and beliefs that govern the types of foods that Jews can and cannot eat: food not aligned with these requirements is called *treifa* (non-kosher). Today kosher is widely used to designate the 'rabbinic properness' or personalised understanding of a wide range of objects, products, activities, ideas and institutions.

As kosher regulation started to increase in the 1990s, Jewish organisations and consumers claimed that while non-Jewish food businesses and management practitioners understood how kosher laws affected their own products, they lacked a deeper understanding of the religious significance that they hold for kosher consumers and rabbis. They argued that this situation warranted increased market regulation and cooperation between Jewish authorities/groups and business/industry. Consequently, kosher is expanding in terms of the number and types of products certified. In the US, many non-Jewish consumers also see kosher as a marker of quality control, which means that competition between the Big Five kosher certification agencies has increased greatly. From the 1990s onwards, the Big Five have largely dominated the global kosher market. At the national level, Israel, the US, the UK and France are important markets for kosher production, trade, regulation and consumption.

Case Study: Kosher in the US

This case is largely based on *Kosher Private Regulation in the Age of Industrial Food* (Lytton 2013).

The US kosher market is an example of successful private-sector regulation in an era of growing public concern over the government's inability to ensure food safety (Lytton 2013). From the 1990s onwards, the Big Five kosher certification agencies not only became dominant in the US, they also started to make inroads into the global kosher market.

- Orthodox Union (OU)
- OK Kosher Certification
- Kosher Certification and Supervision
- Star-K
- Chicago Rabbinical Council

Today more than 10,000 businesses produce kosher food in the US, and this market generates more than $12 billion in annual retail sales.

The US kosher market is an example of how successful private-sector regulation can work successfully in an era of growing public concern over government's inability to ensure food safety at the national and also at the global level. Historically, outbreaks of foodborne illness, fraud, corruption and misleading food labels prompted a network of more than 300 private kosher certifiers throughout the United States to ensure compliance with religious standards of food production and reliable marketing. This case also highlights the emergence of third-party certification that is essential to understanding kosher and halal regulation from the 1990s onwards. Comparing the US kosher market to most other countries where there is a kosher market, one finds that these are less regulated and reminiscent of the US market before the 1990s. The origin of private kosher certification agencies is inseparable from new demands for industrially prepared foods among Jewish consumers around 1900 that spurred a gradual professionalisation of kosher supervision based on ethical standards and increasing bureaucratisation of kosher certification agencies. Unsurprisingly, fraud and misconduct still occur, but today these agencies still utilise social networks to establish and enforce the American standard of kosher certification (Lytton 2013).

In the US kosher is big business, and the country's 10,000 kosher-producing companies make more than 135,000 kosher products for more than 12 million American consumers. Only 8% of kosher consumers are religious Jews, while other consumers choose kosher food for other reasons, notably health, quality and because of its similarity to halal. The growing popularity of kosher food in the US can be seen as a response to cultural anxieties about industrialised food supply and a way of personalising food production. Five features of the market for industrial kosher certification can account for its ability to provide reliable certification:

- sufficient consumer demand
- brand competition among certifiers based on reliability
- a high level of interdependence among certifiers
- concentration of market power between the Big Five
- as well as active and vigilant consumers.

To conclude, this case shows how and why kosher has become a big and regulated business sector in the US. It also demonstrates that business must study the aspects of national kosher markets when producing or marketing kosher products.

Halal literally means 'lawful' or 'permitted' and is based on statements from selected verses and rulings by Islamic scholars (*ulama*). Halal is that which is beneficial and not detrimental to Muslims, and a number of conditions and prohibitions must be observed at all times. These conditions and prohibitions, for example:

- 'Allah makes good things lawful to them and bad things unlawful' (7, 157).
- 'You who believe, eat the good things We have provided for you and be grateful to God, if it is Him that you worship' (2, 172).
- 'He has only forbidden you what dies of itself and blood and flesh of swine and that over which any other name than that of Allah has been invoked, but whoever is driven to necessity, not desiring nor exceeding the limit, then surely Allah is Forgiving, Merciful' (2, 173).

Muslims are expressly forbidden from eating pork and animals that have been killed or slaughtered inappropriately: such substances are called haram – 'unlawful' or 'forbidden'. As well as the proscribed method of slaughter (dhabh) and the ban on pork, there are other requirements relating to specific species of animals. Sea creatures and locusts are generally considered halal – even if they have died spontaneously. Land creatures such as predators, dogs and, in the eyes of some religious scholars, donkeys, are haram. Islamic scholars have also condemned crocodiles, weasels, pelicans, otters, foxes, elephants, ravens and insects: some of these animals are seen as detestable (*makruh*) and are thus not classified as haram *per se*.

Another significant Islamic prohibition relates to wine and any other alcoholic drink or substance, all of which are *haram*. It should be noted however that alcohol has become a highly controversial question for Muslims, not only in relation to drinking but also its use in industrial food production processes. More generally, the understanding and practice of halal requirements vary among countries, regions and companies producing and importing halal products.

In the rapidly expanding global market for halal products Southeast Asia holds a special position. In Indonesia, Malaysia, Singapore and

Brunei state bodies certify halal products and spaces (shops, factories and restaurants) as well as work processes. Globally, companies and certifiers are affected by the proliferation of halal that to a large extent has been brought about by developments in these Southeast Asian nations. In some of these countries, many care products are also halal certified, as are paper/plastic labels and printing on food, which are often seen as problematic. Knowledge of the above requirements is essential to innovative companies trying to establish themselves in the expanding global halal marketplace.

The increased demand for halal products by conscious and educated Muslim consumers globally has also encouraged developed countries to produce and export halal products. In this way, developed countries have entered a market that was previously dominated by Muslim-majority countries in the developing world. Moreover, the proliferation of Western franchised food has changed the international food market and subjected it to new standards of halal certification. In recent years, the ongoing expansion of the halal market has in turn led to the emergence of new standards and certification regimes from countries in the Middle East United Arab Emirates (UAE).

Case Study: Halal in Malaysia

This case is based on *Proper Islamic Consumption* (Fischer 2008) and *The Halal Frontier: Muslim Consumers in a Globalised Market* (Fischer 2011).

Malaysia holds a special position in the rapidly expanding global market for halal products. It is one of the only countries where a state body (Jabatan Kemajuan Islam Malaysia or the Islamic Development Department of Malaysia (JAKIM) regulates halal products, spaces (shops, factories and restaurants) as well as work processes. Over the past three decades, Malaysia has become a world leader in the global expansion of halal markets. This came about in large part because the state and government of Malaysia took on the role of a halal-certifying authority, certifying, standardising and bureaucratising halal production, trade and consumption in a way that made it possible to extend these standards abroad. In shops around the world, consumers can find state halal-certified products from Malaysia that carry distinctive halal logos.

In a wider context, the proliferation of halal is to a large extent evoked by a range of Southeast Asian nations including Singapore, Indonesia and Thailand. Islamic revivalist critiques of 'secularism' and the 'secular state' in Malaysia have helped shape and reinforce a highly commercialised version of Islam, in which halal plays a significant role. Constitutionally, since Malaysia gained independence from Britain in 1957, Malays, the dominant ethnic group in Malaysia, have been classed as Malays only if they are Muslims. Malaysia is not an Islamic state, but Islam is Malaysia's official religion, acknowledged by more than 50% of the population, who for the most part are ethnic Malays.

Since the early 1980s, halal has been institutionalised and regulated by the state in Malaysia. Later reforms included encouragement of competitive advantage in the Malaysian economy by developing niche markets for halal and Islamic products through a vendor system in which companies were tied to government-linked companies controlled by the government and multinationals. These policies were continued through liberalisation of the economy coupled with promoting Malaysia as a hub for halal and Islamic services.

To some extent, Malaysia is also becoming a halal hub for Islamic tourism, with visitors increasing from the Middle East in particular. In the 1970s, the state launched its New Economic Policy (NEP) to improve the economic and social situation of Malays *vis-à-vis* the Chinese minority in particular. The state began regulating halal, and from this it gradually developed the vision to become the world leader in halal production, trade and regulation. It is in this context that the intensified regulation of halal should be seen – for example it is a legal requirement that food-producing/selling businesses must set up a Halal Committee to comply with halal requirements.

Malaysia is a country in which regulatory halal institutions and markets meet. For example, Malaysia has established a national halal assurance system that matches the country's long-term halal strategy incorporating the standards Malaysian MS 1500 (production, preparation, handling and storage of halal food) and MS 2200 (consumer goods for cosmetic and personal care) as an international benchmark for the state certification of halal products.

In sum, halal plays a special role in Malaysia. Many Malays are fastidious about everyday food consumption, and businesses are subjected to strict regulation by the state when producing and marketing not only food but also care products.

Conclusion

Important issues in the literature on kosher and halal concern how regulation in the form of certification, legislation and inspections was tightened as a response to increased awareness among Muslim and Jewish consumers at the global level. The proliferation of religious production methods globally means that it is no longer exclusively Jews or Muslims who are in charge of production, and it is this that has strengthened calls for regulation by trustworthy third-party certification bodies. As we have seen already, kosher and halal share many similarities, but there are also noteworthy differences. It is to these aspects that we now turn.

Bibliography

Fischer, J. (2008) *Proper Islamic Consumption, Shopping Among the Malays in Modern Malaysia*. Copenhagen: Nordic Institute of Asian Studies Press.

Fischer, J. (2011) *The Halal Frontier: Muslim Consumers in a Globalized Market*. New York: Palgrave Macmillan.

Lytton, T. D. (2013) *Kosher Private Regulation in the Age of Industrial Food*. Cambridge: Harvard University Press.

3 Similarities and differences between kosher and halal

Kosher and halal share a number of similarities, including the avoidance of a range of animals, with pigs being the most prominent case: this also means that gelatine and similar substances must also come from permissible animals.

Similarities between kosher and halal

- Pork avoidance
- Similar prohibitions for animals: more are prohibited under kosher laws
- Prohibition of blood
- Avoidance of gelatine and similar substances from unacceptable animals
- Specific requirements during animal slaughter, though these are more contested among Muslims
- Segregation in food supply chain – between meat, dairy and parve (neither meat nor dairy) for kosher, and between halal and non-halal depending on the product/market.

While kosher and halal are similar in these respects, a number of differences can also be observed, which we highlight in what follows and discuss in greater detail in subsequent chapters.

Major differences between kosher and halal

- More species of animals are prohibited in kosher: for example mammals must 'chew the cud' and have cloven hooves.
- Alcohol (beverages and in industrial processes) is allowed in Judaism, but generally this is not the case in Islam.
- Milk and meat must be separated in kosher, while this is not the case with halal: meat and fish are also kept separate in kosher restaurants.

- Kosher has a longer history of regulation/certification than halal. While the Big Five certifiers have systematically regulated the global kosher market from the 1990s onwards, similar trends only started to emerge in the halal market at the start of the new millennium.
- Kosher is generally focused on a wider range of requirements in connection with religious festivals, notably Passover.
- Regulation and certification are organised differently among kosher and halal certifiers.
- Kosher certification bodies generally have a wider remit than halal certification bodies, which have tended to focus on specific sectors (i.e. the meat industry; raw materials; butchers, shops, restaurants and grocery stores).
- Many Muslims would accept kosher, while strictly observant Jews would generally not accept halal.
- Kosher is often considered more 'complex' (for with regard to pollution/contamination from non-kosher production) than halal.
- Because of its longer history of institutionalisation, kosher is often also seen as more 'regulated'.
- In some aspects of kosher production, rabbis are more directly involved than their Muslim counterparts; for example, they are always present when equipment is being cleaned and cleansed.
- Israel, the US, the UK and France are important countries in the global kosher market, while Southeast Asia has been central to the development of the global halal market.

In this book, we consider kosher and halal in the context of societies in which Jews and Muslims are majorities and minorities respectively.

Part II

Central themes and actors

4 Certification, inspections and logos

In this chapter we discuss certification, inspections and logos with a specific focus on how business can address a range of challenges related to the certification process, religious inspection and the design/placement of kosher/halal logos. On kosher/halal production, even if certification, inspections and logos are also important aspects with regard to meat, biotech, shops and restaurants, as we discuss in Part III of the book.

Certification means to state that something is true or 'certain', and certification is thus the most significant transformation in kosher/halal markets over the last three decades or so (in Chapter 6 we discuss different certifiers and how to choose between them). Prior to the age of certification, it was fine for companies to 'self-certify' production, but that time is long past; today, inexpensive certification easily obtained is often considered unreliable and inadequate.

Certification became important in the global kosher market from the 1990s onwards, while this happened around the year 2000 for halal (Lever and Fischer 2018). The reasons for this transformation are many, but three issues stand out. First, a range of food scandals such as BSE in cattle and salmonella in chicken made meat/poultry problematic in food production, and this warranted and enhanced calls for certification. Second, some Jewish/Muslim groups and individuals argued that non-Jewish/Muslim food industries might understand how kosher/halal laws specifically affect their own product without understanding the religious significance that they hold for religious consumers and religious scholars. In effect, this called for increased market regulation and cooperation between religious organisations and industries. Third, during this period, as food markets globalised, food and product ingredients travelled farther and faster than at any previous time in human history. As a result, third-party certification inspections by kosher/halal certifiers became increasingly important to companies. Most companies already received inspection teams from

Table 4.1 Certification: Ten identified kosher and halal challenges and suggested considerations/actions

Challenges	Suggested considerations/actions
1. Choosing one or more certifiers	• Carefully consider which certifiers specialise in your company's product(s)? For example, which certifier(s) have competing companies chosen? • What is the cost of certification, and does the cost of certification vary among certifiers? (Please see Chapter 6 for a discussion of different certifiers.)
2. Documentation	• What sort of documentation does the certifier want or prefer (certificates/contracts/ingredient lists/flowcharts), and what are the implications and needs of the company? • How is this documentation delivered to the certifier? • Is communication electronic? If not, could it be?
3. Lack of recognition between certifiers	• Certifiers compete much like other business organisations, and it is essential to consider which certifiers 'recognise' the certification of other certifiers, as this may restrict or give access to some national/regional/geographic markets and not others (see what follows). • Major certifiers sometimes do not always recognise smaller certifiers that they may consider to be unreliable/unacceptable; knowledge about these issues is essential for businesses.
4. Kosher versus halal	• Kosher and halal certification is similar and while links between the two can be beneficial, differences can also be observed. • Because kosher and halal are similar it is worth considering 'synergies' between certification: if you have one form of certification, how can that make the other easier? • In general, kosher certifiers see themselves as 'stricter' and kosher as more 'complex' than halal, which is often the case in manufacturing companies.
5. Negotiation	• If a certain part of the production process proves to be challenging in terms of certification, bear in mind certifiers are also 'businesses' that are interested in addressing and working out challenges.
6. Problematic ingredients	• If problematic (animal) ingredients are difficult and/or expensive to replace, consider how technology/innovation and handling as well as negotiation can help to address such issues.

7. Appointing and training staff

- Businesses that wish to be or perhaps already are certified should consider appointing staff with specific expertise in and responsibility for kosher and/or halal.
- Many companies have successfully done this by setting up positions such as 'kosher and halal coordinator', benefiting greatly from this organisational change.
- The person in such a role should be the company's expert on kosher and/or halal and be involved in training staff with regard to kosher and/or halal understanding and practice.

8. Alcohol

- Alcohol is an important and sensitive topic in halal production, and companies should be aware of their certifiers' requirements in this area.

9. Audits and inspections

- When companies negotiate certification they should come to an agreement with certifiers about audits and inspections about the following issues: frequency, duration and content; what is it specifically that auditors/inspectors wish to audit/inspect in the business?
- It is also advisable for companies to push certifiers on the specific methods/procedures employed during audits/inspections. Companies must bear in mind that kosher/halal audits/inspections very rarely create conflict, as both certifier and company are interested in establishing and maintaining a mutually beneficial relationship. An important question here is whether inspections are announced or unannounced.
- Kosher and halal audits/inspections should be negotiated when companies and certifiers first discuss the terms of certification.
- Companies should also bear in mind that as kosher and halal are similar in many respects they should consider 'synergies' between the two in terms of audits/inspections in order to avoid double work.
- Pollution and cross-contamination are concerns for certifiers, and companies should bear in mind that a documented high level of 'secular' hygiene can alleviate such 'religious' concerns.
- If certifiers feel that these concerns have been ritual cleansing of equipment and/or premises can be an option.
- Lastly, companies can make clear that they would like audits/inspections to be carried out by the same auditor/inspector in order for the company and certifier to build up a relationship of mutual trust over time.

10. Getting the logo right

- Carefully consider how kosher/halal logos should be placed/presented: on certificates? websites? products?
- What do certifiers and customers say about how logos are presented?
- In most cases certifiers are flexible about the size and placement of logos.

state/local authorities, 'secular' certifiers and customers, but many were also unsure about how religious regulation differed.

It is important to note that in this context, inspections and the appropriate display of kosher/halal logos are important aspects of everyday production, trade and consumption that allow branded messages to be communicated effectively (Bennett and Lagos 2007).

Conclusion

This chapter has demonstrated that although certification, inspections and logos are challenging issues, they are also critical for the communication of branded messages. The ten suggested considerations and actions outlined in Table 4.1 could ideally be 'standardised', and it is to standards that we turn in the next chapter.

Bibliography

Bennett, W. L. and Lagos, T. (2007) Logo logic: The ups and downs of branded political communication, *The ANNALS of the American Academy of Political and Social Science*, 611 (1).

Lever, J. and Fischer, J. (2018) *Religion, Regulation, Consumption: Globalising Kosher and Halal Markets*. Manchester: Manchester University Press.

5 Standards

Kosher and halal compliance hinges on what we call 'practical standards' for the logistics, systems and infrastructure required to enable the development of food and non-food retailing based on religious observance. Reflecting on standards helps regulators and businesses to develop the infrastructure for this kind of retailing in a commercial and cultural environment in which religious observance is not the overriding concern.

Formal halal standards such as those created by Malaysia MS1500 (2004) are unique in the global market for halal. To our knowledge, similar formal standards do not exist for kosher, even if the Big Five kosher certifiers have agreed on an American Standard of kashrut 'practical standards' (www.magentzedek.org).

Broadly speaking, standards can refer to:

- the design and qualities of products
- the proper conduct of states, organisations and individuals
- instruments of control and forms of regulation attempting to generate elements of global order
- persons with certain qualifications, knowledge or skills
- attempts at generating and reinvigorating social norms and directives
- ideas of similarity and uniformity based on rules
- the usual, generally accepted, normal or 'best way' to do things

How are standards understood in the academic literature?

In the academic literature, standards are a way of standardising things or products. For example:

- workers with regard to uniformity and discipline;
- markets in relation to fixed/uniform prices;

- the packaging of products;
- the way in which capitalists behave and use capital;
- standardised methods that produce consistent results;
- the makers of standards such as scientists and technicians;
- consumers as a product of capitalist development;
- socially regulated consumption;
- the environment.

As we observe throughout this book, all these areas are central to kosher and halal production, trade and consumption, for it is through standards that a 'moral economy' is produced and reproduced (Busch 2000).

While a couple of halal standards exist, formal kosher standards are harder to find. Even if this process is slow and uneven, at the global level certifiers and businesses push for more formal kosher and halal standards. However, standards set by the International Organization for Standardization (ISO), for example, about how to organise, what policies to pursue, what kind of services to offer and how to design products, are also indirectly important for kosher and halal production, trade and regulation. Many businesses have complied with 'practical kosher standards' since the 1990s, but these kinds of practical standards have not been addressed so far; this book fills this gap.

An example: a biotech company certified by Orthodox Union (OU) that we worked with started replacing the limited number of animal ingredients in production about twenty years ago due to concerns about bovine spongiform encephalopathy (BSE) and rising kosher requirements. Both factors made animal ingredients undesirable, and the company thus complied with kosher standards, which necessitated a change in ingredients and production processes in connection with replacing porcine gelatine with fish gelatine to produce an immobilised lipase (an enzyme) for edible oils. The replacement of animal ingredients by other ingredients was not only resource demanding and costly, it also generated forms of innovation that benefit the company today. In many ways, non-animal ingredients are less problematic in the globalised market in an era of food scares and rising religious requirements.

As this example makes clear, over the last two decades religious principles have played an important role in shaping knowledge, work processes, and practices in organisations. Formalised standardisation in the form of certification and auditing/inspections by an identifiable certifier such as OU marked the start of systematic kosher regulation. Worldwide, the company has one local coordinator per site. This point shows that standardisation is also about persons (employees and inspectors) who each in their own way possess standardised skills to produce and regulate kosher products, 빵 but also transmit kosher knowledge in order to avoid divergent types of classifications globally.

Training itself can be seen as a standardising process in which learning and disciplining meet (see Chapter 17). It is therefore critical to translate the requirements into standardised systems and terminology that can be understood by all the company's employees who are involved on a daily basis in kosher compliance. This is done by formulating a set of global procedures for kosher that work as centralised and standardised procedures for practice.

An example of such standardised practice is kosherization or ritual cleansing. In some cases, kosher inspectors perform kosherization or ritual cleansing of equipment in addition to the cleaning the company does itself. Kosherization is done after producing the only product that contains milk-based ingredients subject to special kosher rules. The ritual cleansing involves leaving the equipment inactive for 24 hours prior to thorough cleansing with hot water or steam under the supervision of the OU inspector. Kosherization is therefore an example of the compatibility of kosher principles and practices shared by certifier and company.

Standardisation of proper handling and transport are challenging not only for the company but also for companies that supply containers, for example, and again documentation and traceability become essential in making kosher production auditable. Even if no formal kosher standards exist, practical standards have been put in place in this company and in many others.

The company was halal certified around 2000 due to the increased focus on halal from Southeast Asia. This transition was relatively smooth, as many of the standards and experiences from kosher were similar for halal. The company complied with a number of ISO standards and certifications – for example quality, environmental and food safety systems. The company was inspected and audited by several halal certifiers in connection with these types of standards and certifications but also by local authorities and customers in countries where production takes place. The company's global kosher and halal coordinator argued that halal standards similar to those of ISO would be desirable. However, until there are halal standards in place, ISO standards help the production process to run smoothly.

With regard to halal, representatives from a multinational biotech company in Malaysia explained to us that the company chose to focus on internationally recognised good manufacturing and food safety practices instead of the Malaysian MS1500 (2004). This tells us that in some cases formalised and broader types of standards can cover areas central to both kosher and halal production.

In a third biotech company, we were informed that MUI's (Indonesian Ulemas Council) halal requirements are 'very strict' and that their Halal Assurance System complements ISO quality management systems. This was also evident at a Malaysian food manufacturing company, which was ISO 9002 (Quality Management) certified alongside food safety regulations from the Malaysian Ministry of Health. A company representative made the case that when you have this kind of certification JAKIM (Islamic Development Department of Malaysia) inspectors tend to be more 'confident' about issuing halal certificates. If they are not evident, inspectors will ask for much more information.

Singapore's largest supermarket chain, NTUC FairPrice, received its first ISO certificate and food safety certification around the same time in 1993. These types of certification work as platforms and procedures for standardisation and standardised practices in all FairPrice outlets, including halal compliance. FairPrice is now also certified by and the Halal Certification Strategic Unit of MUIS is ISO 9001 certified, which organisations wishing to meet the MUIS standard have to comply with. More recently, the Halal Food Authority (HFA) in the UK acquired formal accreditation from the Emirates Authority for Standardization and Metrology (ESMA) to import halal products into the UAE (UAE 2015). Part of the application process for this new standard included adherence to ISO17065, ISO17021 and ISO9001 standards.

Table 5.1 Standards: Identified kosher and halal challenges and suggested considerations/actions

Challenges	Suggested considerations/actions
Choosing standards	• Carefully consider which standards are best for the markets/countries your company works in/the issues your business face.
	• Consider the wider practical implications in terms of work processes and organisational practices.
	• Consider how different types of standards are aligned with certifiers and how this can affect different aspects of business compliance.
	• In some cases, formalised and broader types of standards can cover areas central to both kosher and halal production.
Implementation	• Training can be a standardising process, notably where learning and disciplining meet.
	• Standards can be implemented by formulating a set of global procedures for work as centralised procedures for practice.

Conclusion

The examples in this chapter show that even if formal kosher and standards are uncommon, ISO standards as well as 'practical standards' condition production, trade and regulation. Businesses working on or thinking of entering kosher and halal markets should consider these issues. Our research shows that formalised standards are also important to retailers and supermarkets in Malaysia and elsewhere. We return to this issue in subsequent chapters.

Bibliography

Busch, L. (2000) The moral economy of grades and standards, *Journal of Rural Studies*, 16, pp. 273–283.

MS1500 (2004) Department of Standards Malaysia (2004) *MS 1500:2004: Halal Food – Production, Preparation, Handling and Storage – General Guidelines (first revision)*, Malaysia, www.jsm.gov.my/ms-1500-2009-halal-food#.WS0JBcaB2V4)

UAE (2015) UAE.S GSO 2055–1 2015, HALAL FOOD – Part 1 General Requirements, https://etrans.esma.gov.ae/English/purchase-standards/pages/standard-details.aspx? Standardid=f6441ba3-c012-e711-9416-005056b821e2

6   Kosher and halal certifiers

This chapter lists and discusses important types of kosher and halal certifiers, as well as the experiences of businesses working with these certifiers. There are many forms of national, regional and local rabbinical authorities and Jewish courts of law offering *kashrut* (Jewish religious dietary laws) services. Similarly, there are many types of halal certifiers at the local, national and global levels.

Kosher certifiers

Rabbinate

In Israel, the Chief Rabbinate has a near monopoly on enforcing kosher laws and certification. To our knowledge, this is the closest one can come to kosher state certification worldwide. Other examples of Rabbinate certifiers are the Rabbinate of the Union of Orthodox Hebrew Congregations London and the Danish Rabbinate, even if this body exists in a country where Judaism plays a modest role. The cost of kosher certification is not always easy to research, but our research shows that certification by the Danish Rabbinate is less expensive compared to the Big Five, for example. The Danish Rabbinate only focuses on the Danish context – certifying Danish companies and products for export.

There is competition between and among Rabbinate certifiers and between these certifiers and the Big Five US/Global bodies not only over the income generated by certification, but also because a certifier such as the Danish Rabbinate is more focused on supporting the Danish private sector and not only on generating income. For example, a Rabbi of the Danish Rabbinate explained to us that he would prefer more Danish companies to be certified by the Danish Rabbinate, as this would cut costs and establish a local relationship between companies in Denmark and the Jewish community. Typically, companies with kosher certification in Denmark export to the US, the UK or Israel. In the US, certification by the Big Five is of particular importance (Lytton 2013).

In sum, it is worth comparing the cost and coverage of local Rabbinate versus Big Five certification in each market where a business operates.

The Big Five

The Big Five have dominated the global kosher market from the 1990s onwards:

- **Orthodox Union (OU)** (www.oukosher.org). OU is the oldest and largest kosher certifying body worldwide. OU is a US community-based organisation that certifies more than 500,000 products in more than ninety countries throughout the world.
- **OK Kosher Certification** (www.ok.org). Based in New York, OK Kosher certifies more than 140,000 products manufactured by over 1500 companies globally, including restaurants in the US.
- **Kosher Certification and Supervision** (www.kok-k.org). Based in New Jersey, US, K of K is yet another US based certifier that has become global in scope.
- **Star-K** (www.star-k.org). Star-K Kosher Certification is based in Baltimore, Maryland, and it certifies thousands of food products and food establishments globally.
- **Chicago Rabbinical Council** (www.crcweb.org). The Chicago Rabbinical Council is based in Chicago, Illinois, and their kosher certification is found around the world.

Despite the global prominence of the Big Five, googling 'kosher certification' and/or 'kosher logos' turns up hundreds if not thousands of results. Individual rabbis and representatives of smaller Jewish groups/congregations often offer certification and issue logos.

In the UK, London together with Manchester are centres for kosher production, trade, regulation and consumption, and in these two cities alone there are numerous certification bodies. As in the US, some of the most well-known certification bodies are connected to local *Beth Din* (rabbinical courts of Jewish law) that have various legal powers and varying degrees of authority on a number of religious matters. In the UK, the London Beth Din (www.klbdkosher.org) and the Manchester Beth Din (http://mbd.org.uk) are perhaps the most well known. But there are also many other individual rabbis and stricter kashrut authorities offering similar services (see www.kashrut.com/agencies/ for a global list of kosher certifiers). As in the US, the cost of certification varies within and across different locations.

Scope of kosher certifiers

Kosher certification bodies often have a much wider remit than their halal counterparts. The globalisation of food production has given large kashrut organisations such as Orthodox Union (OU) and Organized Kashrut (OK) an increasingly significant role in many overlapping areas of food production. In many ways, these organisations act as laboratories that oversee new biotechnological developments in enzyme production, for example, as well as testing and products that attempt to bypass religious requirements (**see Chapter's 10 and 18**).

Summary

The Big Five have dominated global kosher certification since the 1990s and continue to do so. Generally, businesses consider these certifiers easy to work with but also expensive. There is intense competition between many different kosher certifiers at many different levels. Our research shows that generally many companies hold the Big Five in high regard but that they are also considered monopolistic and expensive by smaller certifiers and companies in many instances. Globally, Israel, the US, the UK and France are kosher centres in which the major certifiers are based. It is important that businesses compare cost versus coverage when choosing kosher certification. Businesses should also consider the points raised at the end of Chapter 4.

Halal certifiers

As with kosher, there are hundreds if not thousands of halal certifiers, but arguably the number is growing faster than that of kosher due to the fact that halal certification only became important around 2000 and the market is still expanding rapidly. The number of Muslims is also growing worldwide, and it is now recognised that there is a positive relationship between halal certification and business performance (Syazwan, Chin and Fischer 2017). Here we have classified halal certifiers into state certification agencies, transnational certifiers and private-sector agencies, though these boundaries often blur.

State certification and accreditation

- **Islamic Development Department of Malaysia (JAKIM)** (www.halal.gov.my). Since the early 1980s this body has certified products in Malaysia but also globally, and it is generally considered efficient by businesses. JAKIM recognises many local Muslim halal certifiers around the world.

- **The Islamic Religious Council of Singapore (MUIS)** (www. muis.gov.sg/halal/). Comparable to JAKIM, but more focused on the certification of products imported into Singapore due to the fact that Singapore is not a major food-exporting country. Our research shows that many businesses consider MUIS easy to work with.
- **Ghanim International Corporation (Brunei Darussalam)** (www.brunei-halal.com). Ghanim International Corporation is comparable to MUIS, as Brunei is not a major food-exporting country. Ghanim only started its operations in 2009 and mainly focuses on local business.
- **Indonesian Ulemas Council (MUI)** (www.halalmui.org). Strictly speaking MUI is not a national certifier under the Indonesian state. It was however set up by the Indonesian state in 1975 and is today one of the crucial halal global certifiers. Often businesses find MUI to be very 'religious' and not so easy to work with.

Transnational certifiers

Many state certifiers can be also classified as transnational. However, the International Food and Nutrition Council of America (**IFANCA**) is arguably the leading transnational body: its sister organisation in Europe is the Halal Food Council of Europe (**HFCE**).

- **International Food and Nutrition Council of America (IFANCA)** (www.ifanca.org) was founded in Illinois in 1982 and it cooperates closely with the halal authorities in Malaysia, Singapore and Indonesia that recognise the certification of **IFANCA**.
- **Halal Food Council of Europe (HFCE)** (www.hfce.eu) was founded in Belgium in 2010. Much like IFANCA, HFCE works transnationally and markets itself as an Islamic organisation dedicated to research in the fields of food and nutrition.

Scope of halal certifiers

To a large extent, the scope of halal certifiers is not as wide as that of the major kosher certification bodies, though this may be starting to change. If we look just at the UK, we see a wide range of divergent interests and specialisms for individual halal certification bodies. The Halal Food Authority (HFA) (www.halalfoodauthority.eu) has attempted to cover many parts of the market in recent decades but is still largely known for its work with meat producers and slaughter facilities. The Halal Monitoring Committee (https://halalhmc.org) (HMC) is similarly recognised for its work with restaurants, grocery stores and butcher shops, while the Muslim Food Board (www.tmfb.net) focuses on food processing, cosmetics and pharmaceuticals. The Halal Food Council of Europe (HFCE), registered in Belgium but operating transnationally across the UK and other jurisdictions, largely focuses on the export of raw materials and is thus generally more engaged in enzyme certification than most of these bodies.

Recent developments

Until recently, the major certifiers in Southeast Asia played a central role in the global market for halal-certified products. They still do to a large extent, and they are widely recognised by all the major transnational certifiers. In recent years, however, change has in the global market as new standards and certifiers have begun to emerge in the Gulf states and across the Middle East. These include most notably **The Emirates Authority for Standardization and Metrology (ESMA)** in the United Arab Emirates (UAE).

The UAE is the first country in the Middle East to regulate halal certificates and logos for all halal food products. **ESMA** was established as the sole standardisation body in the UAE, and it now oversees the work of the **Dubai Accreditation Department (DAC)** (www.dac.dm.ae/dac/major/home) and other certification bodies in the region. In the last few years, this has created tension in the global market, as certifiers in different national and regional contexts have been forced to renegotiate relationships with their business partners in order to retain market access. Businesses need to be aware of the dynamic nature of the certification relationships involved across different countries and regions, which can change at short notice.

Case Study: Halal food authority – changing market requirements

The Halal Food Authority (HFA) (www.halalfoodauthority.eu) is the oldest halal certification body in the UK. It was the first organisation in the UK to grant licenses to businesses in line with inspections and audits that assessed compliance with Islamic principles alongside UK and EU regulation. Initially, the HFA certified un-stunned meat as halal. However, as the market grew and the organisation became established as the major halal certification body in the UK, it began to accept pre-slaughter stunning, as this aligned them more closely with mainstream scientific practice and animal welfare considerations emanating from UK and EU policy (Lever and Miele 2012).

During this period, HFA also built relationships with some of the leading global halal certifiers, including JAKIM in Malaysia (www.islam.gov.my). In recent years, as the United Arab Emirates (UAE) and other Gulf states have started to enter the global market, the HFA has had to renegotiate many of its business relationships at the national and global level to comply with the demands and requirements of the Emirates Authority for Standardization and Metrology (ESMA). The HFA's formal accreditation to UAE 2055–1 standard (UAE 2015) includes an assessment of quality-management systems, technical audit protocols and adherence to ISO17065, ISO17021 and ISO9001 standards.

Through UAE 2055–2, the UAE is implementing a policy that requires all imported halal products to be certified by bodies accredited and registered with ESMA. In principle, all halal products going into the UAE must come from non-stunned animals, and to protect market access the HFA quickly made the decision to develop and offer certification for meat from non-stun 'traditional halal slaughter' (HFA 2016). These developments came at very short notice, and many businesses working with the HFA faced increasing business compliance and regulatory pressures, as noted by speakers at the HFA Halal Industry Conference in 2016. Almost fifty certification bodies in twenty-four countries were registered with ESMA early in 2018, and the number continues to increase.

Summary

Around the world one can find a plethora of local halal certifiers, often in the form of an Imam or mosque that can certify at a lower cost than the big state and transnational certifiers. However, the coverage of local certification is limited, and businesses should consider their needs carefully before deciding on one or more halal certifiers. Moreover, the major certifiers recognise smaller certifiers on and on and off basis, so it

Table 6.1 Certifiers: Identified kosher and halal challenges and suggested considerations/actions

Challenges	Suggested considerations/actions
Cost and Coverage	• Major certifiers can be expensive • The cost of local certifiers is often lower than transnational certifiers, but coverage may be limited. • Businesses should carefully consider what their needs are, and which markets they want to access before choosing their certification partners.
Change	• Change occurs in line with national and regional politics/policies and wider global developments. • Businesses should consult the websites of the major certifiers regularly to keep abreast of current developments.

is always advisable to consult the websites of the major certifiers for the latest update.

Conclusion

When choosing a kosher/halal certifier, businesses should consider the points raised here and at the end of Chapter 4 carefully.

Bibliography

HFA (2016) *Fact Sheet – HFA Certification of Traditional Halal Slaughter (without stunning)*. London and Toumai: Halal Food Authority. http://halalfoodauthority.com/fact-sheet, acessed 10 October 2016.

Lever, J. and Fischer, J. (2018) *Religion, Regulation, Consumption: Globalising Kosher and Halal Markets*. Manchester: Manchester University Press. Halal Food Authority, http://halalfoodauthority.com/fact-sheet, accessed 24 October 2016.

Lever J. and Miele, M. (2012) The growth of Halal meat markets in Europe: An exploration of the supply side theory of religion, *Journal of Rural Studies*, 28 (4), pp. 528–537.

Lytton, T. D. (2013) *Kosher Private Regulation in the Age of Industrial Food*. Cambridge: Harvard University Press.

Syazwan, M. T., Chin, T. I. and Fischer, J. (2017) Linking Halal food certification and business performance, *British Food Journal*, 119 (7), pp. 1606–1618.

UAE (2015) UAE.S GSO 2055–1 2015, HALAL FOOD – Part 1 General Requirements, https://etrans.esma.gov.ae/English/purchase-standards/pages/standard-details.aspx? Standardid=f6441ba3-c012-e711-9416-005056b821e2

7   Government

In this chapter we look briefly at the role played by governments and state authorities around the globe. Outside Israel governments are not really involved in the kosher market, and outside Southeast Asia the same can largely be said of halal. In the UK, and across Europe more generally, the only national regulation related to kosher and halal production occurs at the time of killing during animal slaughter (Lever and Miele 2012; see also Chapter 9). However, in most non-Muslim countries our research suggests that many producing and exporting businesses would like to see more government involvement, particularly when exporting products to markets in which kosher and/or halal are important (Lever and Fischer 2018).

There are some examples of good practice in this area. In Malaysia, the Danish state is actively involved in assisting Danish companies in halal matters through embassy representation, but this involvement is fairly recent, and not all businesses are aware of this service. The Commercial Section of the Danish Embassy in Kuala Lumpur, for example, offers its services to Danish companies that operate or want to operate in Malaysia. The Embassy has employed a local Malaysian advisor responsible for agro-based industries, halal food and consumer/retail products. Malaysia's halal certification and logo are not only important for companies operating in Malaysia, they are also recognised within the Association of Southeast Asian Nations (ASEAN) as well as globally; this poses challenges for Danish companies and also for Denmark as a country that exports a high volume of agro-based products.

Denmark recognises the importance of deepening halal understanding and practice – especially in connection with abattoirs and the export of food products for Muslim countries and groups. Abattoirs in Denmark have halal inspections every two to three years by the Department of Veterinary Services in Malaysia together with JAKIM. These bodies send officers to Denmark to check that poultry are slaughtered properly according to Islamic principles, for example, while the Malaysian Embassy tries to assist Danish companies that find Malaysian halal requirements complex. In addition to the processing fee imposed by Department of Veterinary Services in Malaysia, the companies inspected in Denmark must cover travel expenses when these agencies visit Denmark. Similarly, but at a lower cost, Danish companies must pay the JAKIM-accredited Islamic Cultural Centre (ICC) in Denmark for certification, labelling of products with logos and inspections. Similar developments are evident in other countries.

There are powerful linkages in and between governments globally, and it is essential that businesses explore these avenues in their respective countries to see what state support is available. Support has been limited until now, but as the halal market in particular continues to expand this is starting to change.

Bibliography

Lever, J. and Fischer, J. (2018) *Religion, Regulation, Consumption: Globalising Kosher and Halal Markets.* Manchester: Manchester University Press.

Lever J. and Miele, M. (2012) The growth of Halal meat markets in Europe: An exploration of the supply side theory of religion, *Journal of Rural Studies*, 28 (4), pp. 528–537.

8 Consumers

There is now a fairly detailed body of research exploring how Jewish and Muslim consumers understand and practice kosher and halal globally (Fischer 2008, 2011; Bergeaud-Blackler, Lever and Fischer 2015; Lever and Fischer 2017). Obviously, Jewish and Muslim consumers are comprised of extremely diverse groups based on gender, age, education/occupation and ethnicity. However, based on existing research some general findings can be identified. In what follows we outline a fourfold typology of consumers:

Four types of (Muslim/Jewish) consumers

1. The fastidious/observant/orthodox

These consumers are very focused on kosher/halal, and they will only eat religiously acceptable food: it is also typical within this group that kosher/halal is about much more than food – for example, care products, toothpaste, brushes without pig's hair and acceptable forms of Islamic finance. This group of consumers look carefully for logos on products and inspect them carefully; they may also call help lines, use smartphone apps or approach contacts at their local synagogue or mosque to clarify any anxieties or concerns that they may have about certain products. In sum, these consumers understand and practice their religion through consumption and vice versa, that is, everyday consumption is an expression of religion and spirituality.

2. The commonsense or pragmatic consumers

This group is aware that kosher/halal are religious injunctions, and they are concerned about these requirements, at least rhetorically. If kosher/halal are readily available at the right price they may buy it, but it's not absolutely essential in their everyday lives. In sum, these consumers are pragmatic about their everyday consumption and religious observance – they do not consistently equate religion with consumption. They may purchase certified kosher or halal products from a variety of sources, including local butcher shops as well as mainstream supermarkets and fast food restaurants.

3. Rebels

These are Muslims/Jews that reject kosher/halal as overly orthodox. These consumers will argue that it's always up to the individual to decide whether kosher/halal is important to them and that the certification of these products is not only a case of market excess but also an expression of power for businesses and certifiers alike.

4. Non-Muslim/Jewish consumers

Our research shows that most non-Muslim/Jewish consumers are not really worried about buying kosher/halal products. Very often, consumers are not even aware that products in supermarkets carry a kosher and/ or halal logo. It should also be noted that the classification of consumers outlined above is a simplification, and that kosher/halal understanding and practice will often overlap and change in and between these groups.

Case Study: kosher and halal consumption

The context of consumption is important for consumer behaviour in at least two respects. Firstly, the availability of kosher and halal products conditions consumption. Secondly, the religious/secular setting also impacts consumer behaviour.

With regard to kosher, our study (Lever and Fischer 2018) of kosher and halal in the UK proves this point. There is wide availability of kosher products in cities such as London and Manchester due to a strong Jewish presence. Peter, in his thirties with three children, works as an accountant in Manchester. He received education at a prominent Jewish school in London and spent two years in Israel, and he frequently goes to the local synagogue. Peter argues that food is kosher only if it complies with the Jewish dietary laws of *kashrut* and the family applies this in the home, where they have a kosher kitchen with two sinks, two dishwashers and two ovens to keep it 'neutral for meat and milk', and also outside the house when they go to a restaurant. All the places they eat must have a certificate stating that the food is formally kosher, and *kashrut* is thus central to their everyday food practice. Peter acknowledges that some Jewish people will say they 'keep kosher' but will be nowhere near as strict as he is. For Peter, however, kosher is all-encompassing. When he organises family events, for example, or entertains clients at work, he always orders the food from prominent kosher restaurants in his own neighbourhood. Having children also reinforced his desire to pass knowledge of kosher on to the next generation. Food consumption, for Peter, is a direct reflection of piety: 'I think it's a very important part of it actually . . . people say blessings before we have the foods, you know. You shouldn't be sort of gluttonous.' This is a big part of the community, and he notes that a lot of Jewish events are based around food.

Omar is in his thirties with three children and of Pakistani descent. He studied medicine at the University of Manchester and now works in a medical centre in the city. Omar attends his local mosque regularly, where he is a trustee. If stunning leads to death before the proper halal procedure has been completed during meat production – and it is his understanding that most stunning does hinder such practice – this renders the meat haram and therefore unsuitable for Muslim consumption. All the necessary conditions have to be fulfilled to make meat halal, and Omar argues that humane slaughter is thus central to Islamic practice. Other important areas in halal food production relate to ingredients added to pre-prepared food. If a product has no prohibited ingredients, which is usually the case with vegetarian food, Omar argues that such food is permissible. Regarding the acceptability of small amounts of questionable ingredients in food products, he states that for him personally this is unacceptable; he gives the example of gelatine and states that there is now enough choice for Muslims to avoid it permanently and 'stay safe'. In relation to non-food products such as toothpaste, Omar feels that there is a need for halal alternatives. Omar wants his children to grow up understanding what halal is and what they can and cannot eat at school.

Other Jewish and Muslim informants have quite a different view on the above fastidiousness: they either reluctantly accept the imposition of religion/consumption or simply reject it as a material and thus shallow display of belief – as religious materialism or excess. Interestingly, the relationship outlined in this chapter between the fastidious/observant/orthodox on the one hand and the rebels on the other hand can be seen in all societies with Jewish and Muslim populations.

The following factors condition kosher/halal understanding and practice:

- Women are often in charge of shopping and cooking, and thus they are often seen to be responsible for ensuring religiously acceptable food in households and families. Interestingly, it is typically men who act responsible for kosher/halal production, trade and regulation.
- In countries and regions where kosher/halal are promoted and/or regulated by the state, consumers are influenced by powerful arguments about kosher/halal being an important, healthy, patriotic and proper expression of religious life, perhaps more so in the case of halal in South East Asia than elsewhere.
- Especially with regard to modern halal, over the last two decades or so there has been a radical transformation towards certification and logos on products, in advertisements and on websites. This has made millions of consumers aware that the religious quality of products can now be assessed more easily.
- Many consumers rely on information disseminated by religious organisations as well as by rabbis and imams. Telephone help lines, websites and smartphone apps are also becoming increasingly popular as a way of assessing and clarifying product compliance.
- To a large extent, although this can vary by location, the most orthodox Jewish consumers are more orthodox than their Muslim counterparts. While there are often other historical and geographical factors involved, including the pre-existence of minority communities, this often means that while many Muslim consumers will accept kosher food, fewer Jewish consumers accept halal certification.

- In relation to halal, a growing global Muslim middle class is emerging, and this group tends to be more focused on halal, which arguably helps to explain why/how halal has grown exponentially over the last two decades or so. Generally, many middle-class consumers are just as focused on health and nutrition as they are religious requirements and spirituality, so businesses should consider both aspects.
- Kosher and halal are often inseparable from urban spaces and urbanisation: it is in urban spaces such as super/hypermarkets that kosher/halal products are produced, marketed and regulated.

Conclusion

Businesses should always take the points outlined above into consideration. They should always remember that kosher/halal understanding and practice are more often than not context specific, and that careful analysis of context should always be taken into consideration by businesses when entering different regional markets.

Bibliography

Bergeaud-Blackler, F., Lever, J. and Fischer, J. (eds) (2015) *Halal Matters: Islam, Politics, and Markets in Global Perspective*. New York: Routledge.

Fischer, J. (2008) *Proper Islamic Consumption: Shopping Among the Malays in Modern Malaysia*. Copenhagen: Nordic Institute of Asian Studies Press.

Fischer, J. (2011) *The Halal Frontier: Muslim Consumers in a Globalized Market*. New York: Palgrave Macmillan.

Lever, J. and Fischer, J. (2017) *Religion, Regulation, Consumption: Globalising Kosher and Halal Markets*. Manchester: Manchester University Press.

Part III
Case studies in context

9 Meat and poultry production

Historically meat has been the primary concern of kosher and halal consumers, and to a large extent this is still the case today. Jews and Muslims have similar religious requirements for meat, and in recent decades production has been lifted out of its traditional religious base in both markets. In the UK, for example, as well as being sold in local butcher shops, kosher and halal meat are now also widely available in super/hypermarkets, mainstream restaurants and public institutions (see Chapters 14, 15 and 16).

To avoid misuse and ensure compliance to Jewish and Islamic legal practice, tighter regulation has emerged. Stunning – the process through which animals are rendered immobile or unconscious prior to slaughter – is a central and contentious issue in kosher and halal meat production for both religious and non-religious consumers. While all kosher meat is produced without stunning animals before slaughter, halal meat production is far more complex; while some Muslims accept stunning, others do not.

Kosher meat

The original requirements for the production of kosher meat emerge from specific passages in the Torah (specifically Exodus, Leviticus and Deuteronomy) and in texts linked to the Talmud. Pig meat is specifically prohibited, and Jews are only permitted to consume the meat of animals that 'chew the cud' and have 'cloven hooves', for example, cattle, sheep and goats. There are also prohibitions against eating certain types of birds and fowl: chicken, turkey, duck and goose are the most commonly consumed. Meat and poultry can *only* be kosher if the animal of origin is slaughtered using appropriate methods (*shechita*) as interpreted through rabbinic commentaries and traditional customary practice. Non-stun *schecita* slaughter is the universally practiced method of slaughter, which is discussed in detail in the Talmud.

Three principles must be followed at all times (Lytton 2013).

1. *Only* suitably qualified and skilled Jewish slaughterers (*schoctim*) with the required knowledge and understanding of Jewish law can conduct slaughter.
2. Slaughter must be carried out with a razor-sharp blade on a special knife (a *Chalaf*) to minimise the risk of damage to the body of the animal being slaughtered; the knife must be well maintained to avoid bad practice.
3. The cut (the act of slaughter) requires a smooth *to* and *fro* motion across a clearly defined part of the animal's neck; any mistake in this action and the animal carcass is rendered non-kosher (or *treifa*). The Talmud also outlines a Hebrew blessing that must be recited prior to the act of slaughter.

After slaughter, a specially trained expert must conduct an inspection of the animal carcass to check for any signs of illness or injury. As the most commonly damaged organs, the lungs of cattle are inspected for damage that would render them unfit (*treifa*) under Jewish law; the intestines of poultry are checked in a similar way. If the lungs are free of injuries the meat is termed *glatt* – a Yiddish word meaning smooth; if they are not, they can still be kosher but not *glatt*.

As kosher production has industrialised in the US and rabbinate supervising industrial plants have come under increasing pressure, *glatt* has become more important (Lytton 2013); the Orthodox Union (OU) now refers to *glatt* as a higher standard of kosher. Our research suggests that in places such as London and Manchester in the UK, some smaller certification bodies focus solely on this higher standard, including the Machzikei Hadass Kashrut Board. Others, such as the London Board for Shechita (www.shechita.org), certify *glatt* alongside regular kosher (Lever and Fischer 2018).

Kosher meat certification versus supervision

Certification occurs when a factory or restaurant complies with kosher requirements in all aspects of production. In this situation, there will be no non-kosher production on site, and everything produced will be classed as kosher and therefore certified as such. Alternatively, when a company makes a particular batch of products for the kosher market this is a supervised relationship. With the former, costs are lower, because after the initial inspection there is no need for a supervisor to be on site to oversee production. With the latter, there will be a full-time kosher representative on site during production, and there will be costs associated with clean-ing and cleansing equipment, for example, which will make the overall process much more expensive (Lever and Fischer 2018).

Case Study: The Manchester Beth Din

The Manchester Beth Din (www.mbd.org.uk) (MBD) has a long history stretching back to 1892. Prior to this, synagogues act-ing under individual rabbinical authority provided *kashrut* and *shechita* services across Manchester, and today some of MBD's most important functions still revolve around similar activities for slaughterhouses, manufacturers and butchers. In recent dec-ades, the Manchester Beth Din has also become established at the international level. The organisation supervises companies in Europe, the United States, China, India and Japan, amongst other places, and they now oversee *shechita* in Poland, Hungary and Romania. MBD certified kosher meat is sold and supplied in unprocessed and manufactured forms in a number of Euro-pean countries, notably where non-stun slaughter is prohibited or banned. At the start of the MBD certification or supervision process, companies are asked to fill out an application form. All raw ingredients used in production must be disclosed before stor-age, production and packing areas are inspected, and a full audit is undertaken. Only when everything is in order will a contract be agreed and signed (see page 48).

Halal meat

The original food rulings and dietary laws underpinning the produc-tion of halal meat emerge from specific passages in the Qur'an. As in the kosher meat market, certain conditions and prohibitions must be observed and practiced at all times:

- Muslims must not consume pork or any porcine derivatives, as all such substances are *haram* and therefore 'unlawful' or 'forbidden'.
- In all instances, the lawfulness of meat depends on how it is obtained and how animals are slaughtered; animals that have suffered injury, death or illness are strictly prohibited.

Kosher approval process

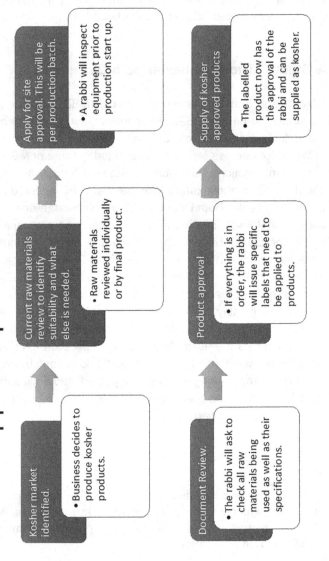

Kosher market identified.
- Business decides to produce kosher products.

Current raw materials review to identify suitability and what else is needed.
- Raw materials reviewed individually or by final product.

Apply for site approval. This will be per production batch.
- A rabbi will inspect equipment prior to production start up.

Document Review.
- The rabbi will ask to check all raw materials being used as well as their specifications.

Product approval
- If everything is in order, the rabbi will issue specific labels that need to be applied to products.

Supply of kosher approved products
- The labelled product now has the approval of the rabbi and can be supplied as kosher.

This is a standard kosher approval process identified during the course of our research.

- Prior to halal slaughter (*Dhabh*) animals must be clean and healthy, well fed and watered; they must be treated gently, and at the time of slaughter they must be calm.
- A Muslim must conduct the act of slaughter with a cut to a clearly defined area of the neck with a regularly inspected and maintained sharp knife.
- The slaughterer must recite an appropriate Islamic blessing over each animal or bird at the time of slaughter.
- All blood must be allowed to drain from the body of the animal post-slaughter, and death must be caused by exsanguination (bleeding). The slaughtered animal must not be disturbed until dead.

For Muslims, the question of stunning is highly contested, and what *Dhabh* slaughter actually entails in practice is under constant discussion by scholars, imams and consumers, particularly in non-Muslim countries. These discussions originate in debates about the origins of Islam, which Muslims believe are derived from two sources – the Qur'an and Sunnah (the teachings, sayings and practices of the prophet Muhammad). Attitudes towards stunning also differ across the four schools of jurisprudence (*Madh'habs*) within Sunni Islam – the Hanafi, Hanbali, Maliki and Shafie schools – and also within schools within Shia Islam (see Bergeaud-Blackler, Lever and Fischer 2015).

These differences are also reflected in the policies of certification bodies. For example, when Malaysia launched the first global halal standard for halal food in 2004 – which provides certification for the production, preparation, handling and storage of halal food (Department of Standards Malaysia 2004) – stunning was not recommended. In 2009, however, as the global halal market was starting to expand, the standard was revisited, and a commitment was made to accommodate pre-slaughter stunning under certain conditions, most notably for poultry (Department for Standards Malaysia 2009).

More changes have occurred in recent years as countries in the Middle East have entered the global market. Notably, the Emirates Authority for Standardization and Metrology (ESMA) (www.esma.gov.ae), which prioritises non-stun slaughter over pre-stun slaughter, is becoming a major player. As noted in previous chapters, requirements for certification, inspection and production practices are changing in line with these developments, and our research suggests that this can be costly and time consuming for businesses (Lever and Fischer 2018).

In many non-Muslim countries, there are now certification bodies specialising in meat from both un-stunned and pre-stunned animals (Bergeaud-Blackler et al 2015). In the European Union, legislation

Table 9.1 Halal accreditation with country/regional standard setting body for HFA and HMC

	Malaysia	Indonesia	Singapore	UAE
	JAKIM	*MUI*	*MUIS*	*ESMA*
Halal Food Authority (HFA)	Yes	Yes	Yes	Yes
Halal Monitoring Committee (HMC)	No	No	No	Yes

requires that all animals are stunned prior to slaughter. However, derogation from this legislation allows minority groups to practice non-stun slaughter in line with religious freedoms granted in line with Article 10 of the Charter of Fundamental Rights of the European Union. This is interpreted differently by individual member states. While non-stun slaughter (both halal and kosher) is banned in some countries, including Denmark, in countries such as the UK with large Muslim populations, there are now effectively dual markets for halal meat from both stunned and non-stunned animals (Lever and Miele 2012).

Halal meat certification in the UK

The major certifier of pre-stunned halal meat in the UK is the Halal Food Authority (HFA) (www.halalfoodauthority.com). Established in 1994 it is widely recognised by all the major international and transnational certifiers. Once an application is received to license a factory, the HFA undertakes an inspection and conducts an audit of the production methods and labelling procedures to assess a company's compliance with Islamic principles and UK and EU legislation. When this process is completed a fee is paid and the factory receives an annual license and certificate that entitles it to use the HFA logo. As part of the contract, the HFA can make a number of unannounced annual inspections in any one-year period. Any change in the manufacture of meat in terms of processing, patenting and marketing must be communicated immediately to the HFA.

The HFA has an independent board of scholars and ulemas providing guidance on certification and they recently established an impartiality committee, which has key members from academia and industry (e.g. from the AHDB Beef and Lamb Board, www.beefandlamb.ahdb.org.uk) to minimise conflicts of interests. As the market has started to change in recent years in line with the emergence of new transnational certifiers, the HFA has announced a new certification process for producing non-stunned halal meat.

Halal approval process

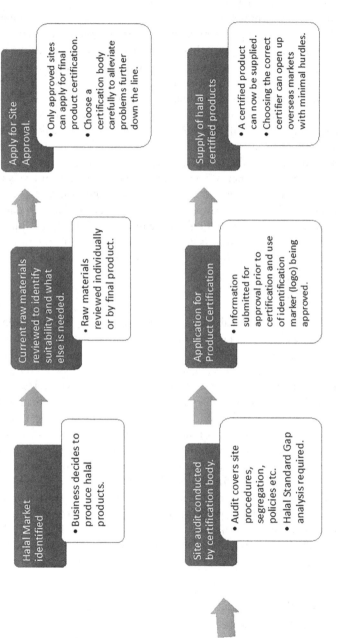

Halal Market identified
- Business decides to produce halal products.

Current raw materials reviewed to identify suitability and what else is needed.
- Raw materials reviewed individually or by final product.

Apply for Site Approval.
- Only approved sites can apply for final product certification.
- Choose a certification body carefully to alleviate problems further down the line.

Site audit conducted by certification body.
- Audit covers site procedures, segregation, policies etc.
- Halal Standard Gap analysis required.

Application for Product Certification
- Information submitted for approval prior to certification and use of identification marker (logo) being approved.

Supply of halal certified products
- A certified product can now be supplied.
- Choosing the correct certifier can open up overseas markets with minimal hurdles.

This is a standard halal approval process identified during the course of our research.

Figure 9.2 Standard halal approval process for certification

The major certifier of non-stunned halal meat in the UK is the Halal Monitoring Committee (HMC) (www.halalhmc.org). Although the HMC does not recognise the legitimacy of many international certification/accreditation bodies, it has still built relationships with many multinational companies operating in the UK (Lever and Miele 2012). As Figure 9.1 illustrates, HMC has recently been recognised by ESMA in the Middle East in line with their new focus on non-stun slaughter; the HFA has also moved into this market. HMC insists on a personal and physical inspection at all slaughterhouses and requires and demands access to all areas of production at all times. An initial visit is usually followed by an audit to see if the company's processes are compatible with HMC's certification requirements. This involves an examination of levels of production, what the risk is and an assessment of how many inspections will be necessary. Third-party inspectors are employed full time to check that halal slaughter is conducted effectively in line with HMCs requirements; this requires that slaughter is carried out by a Muslim, that no stunning equipment is used and that no cross-contamination occurs.

Conclusion

Entering kosher and halal meat markets is a complex undertaking for businesses. Companies need to make sure that they comply with all meat market legislation and certification requirements in each region they wish to work in. Our research suggests that businesses can encounter problems when international practices and standards change quickly and/or new certification bodies and regulatory requirements appear in the market. In this context, national certification bodies such as the HFA in the UK have to adapt to changing market conditions, and this can have a knock-on effect in terms of increased costs for the businesses they in turn certify: the points made at the end of Chapter 4 are relevant here. While halal in particular is boosting fresh meat performance (Alieva 2015), our research also suggests that Jewish and Muslim consumers are increasingly aware of and concerned about the environmental problems associated with the over-production and consumption of meat, dairy and poultry (Lever and Fischer 2018). All such issues will play a central role in the future of kosher and halal food markets, and businesses must be aware of these emerging issues and opportunities.

Bibliography

Alieva, A. (2015) Halal boosts fresh meat performance, *Doing Business in the Halal Market: Products, Trends and Growth Opportunities*. London: Euromonitor International.

Bergeaud-Blackler, F., Lever, J. and Fischer, J. (eds) (2015) *Halal Matters: Islam, Politics, and Markets in Global Perspective*. New York: Routledge.

Department of Standards Malaysia (2004) *MS 1500:2004: Halal Food – Production, Preparation, Handling and Storage – General Guidelines (first revision)*, Malaysia, www.jsm.gov.my/ms-1500-2009-halal-food#.WS0JBcaB2V4

Department of Standards Malaysia (2009) *MS 1500:2009: Halal Food – Production, Preparation, Handling and Storage – General Guidelines (second revision)*, Malaysia, www.jsm.gov.my/ms-1500-2009-halal-food#.WS0JBcaB2V4

Lever, J. and Fischer, J. (2018) *Religion, Regulation, Consumption: Globalising Kosher and Halal Markets*. Manchester: Manchester University Press.

Lever, J. and Miele, M. (2012) The growth of Halal meat markets in Europe: An exploration of the supply side theory of religion, *Journal of Rural Studies*, 28 (4), pp. 528–537.

Lytton, T. D. (2013) *Kosher Private Regulation in the Age of Industrial Food*. Cambridge: Harvard University Press.

10 Biotech production

Introduction

Fermentation has long been used in food production as a way of enhancing and increasing the performance of food. Several food products of historical significance that consumers use regularly today – alcohol, vinegar, cheese and bread, for example – are products of biotechnology. Recent advances in the underlying processes have facilitated the expansion of biotechnology in the food industry, notably in relation to enzymes found in different microorganisms. This chapter explores the implications of these developments in the global markets for kosher and halal food.

Traditionally the majority of enzymes used in the food industry were from animal sources. In relation to kosher and halal this presented many potential problems in terms of tracing and testing for unacceptable animal-based ingredients. In recent years, kosher and halal production has moved beyond meat towards biotechnology for the production and certification of GMOs and enzymes for a wide range of food and drink products. In contemporary global kosher and halal industries biotechnology is becoming an important way of avoiding substances that may be contaminated with porcine (swine) residues (kosher/halal) and/or alcohol (halal) (Blech 2008; Riaz and Chaudry 2004). The primary benefit of biotech production is that it allows microbial enzymes to be produced under controlled conditions (Blech 2008) in laboratories. This has significant implications, not least because in an era of food scares and rising religious requirements non-animal ingredients are less problematic in the globalised market than ingredients derived from animal sources. However, while Jewish and Islamic scholars now accept that products made from simple genetic engineering can be kosher and/or halal, both communities have not yet determined the status of more complex genetic manipulations underpinning the use of GMOs (Blech 2008; Riaz and Chaudry 2004; Lever and Fischer 2018).

Kosher and halal biotech

As meat cannot be mixed with dairy under *kashrut* and *halacha* law, enzymes derived from the stomach lining of animals pose potential problems in kosher biotech (Blech 2008). The manager of a kosher shop in Manchester explained the significance of these developments during the course of our research when discussing yoghourts and cheese sold in the shop (Lever and Fischer 2018). Until forty or fifty years ago, he pointed out that there was no mass production of yoghurts and that for many years producers just let milk turn into yoghurt naturally. Today, however, he pointed out that some producers simply buy yeast off the shelf, and that as far as kosher is concerned the question is no longer simply '*what's the source of the product?*' or '*what animal do these ingredients come from?*' but rather '*what media were they grown on?*' Under these manufacturing conditions, production methods must still be kosher and halal, as must ingredients and processing methods (Lever and Fischer 2018). Commercial decisions by a significant number of biotech food companies to have products designated as kosher and/or halal have thus created a secondary market of auditing and certification companies.

In the global era, non-animal ingredients have thus come to play an important role shaping new knowledge, work processes and certification practices in global kosher and halal markets. Some of the major concerns in halal biotech emerge around dairy production, which we look at in the next chapter. Here we briefly look briefly at the opportunities these developments present for the new knowledge processes involved in production.

During the course of our research (Lever and Fischer 2018), we encountered an innovative enzyme-producing company in the UK certified by both the Manchester Beth Din (MBD) and the Halal Food Council of Europe (HFCE). Rabbis from MBD have been overseeing the production of kosher enzymes at the company for over three decades, and similar practice has emerged more recently in the case of halal. For a long time, the company produced enzymes in the traditional way, from animal sources that had been certified by kosher and halal bodies respectively. In recent decades, however, continuing global growth in both markets has brought about new demands, and the company recently applied for and achieved kosher accreditation from MBD for a new manufacturing facility. The company now has a bioreactor for fermentation on site where they produce and package enzyme blends in line with the requirements of a broad range of companies in global markets. All enzymes produced at the new facility, for individual customers and for the general market, can be kosher, halal or vegetarian, and the company claim that this offers customers a strong competitive advantage.

The move away from animal enzymes to microbial alternatives has been significant for the company, and they have recently produced new commercial enzyme applications. Understanding the developing requirements of religious accreditation has allowed the company to be recognised as one of the world's leading specialty enzyme manufacturers. These developments are also setting new scientific standards for production, preparation, handling, storage and certification of kosher and halal products (Fischer 2015a, 2015b; Lever and Fischer 2018). This requires formalised standardisation in the form of certification and auditing/inspections by identifiable kosher and halal certifiers (see Chapter 5).

Similar developments were evident at a leading global manufacturer of enzymes based in Denmark, which has offices and production facilities in a number of countries. The company has been certified kosher by the OU since the late 1980s, yet in order to comply with the divergent halal requirements that have emerged in recent decades, the company's products have since been certified by five different halal certifiers. The company makes around 900 enzyme products for companies manufacturing detergents, foods, beverages, textiles, biofuel and animal feed, among other things. With a few exceptions, the company's enzymes are all kosher and halal certified, though a greater number are kosher certified because some are for the production of alcoholic beverages.

The company's history of kosher certification has helped them to comply with rising halal requirements in recent decades. This is a more complex area, and a lot of effort is needed to ensure that the requirements of Southeast Asian halal certifiers such as MUI and JAKIM and their recognised halal certification partners in other parts of the world are met. The company train all staff involved in halal production in a similar way, and in relation to halal in particular, training helps certifiers to communicate their specific requirements when getting products and production processes through various certification requirements (see Chapter 17).

Conclusion

Biotech production is creating new opportunities for companies wishing to enter global kosher and halal markets. It is also creating new scientific standards for the production, preparation, handling, storage and certification of kosher and halal products. Businesses aiming to work in these markets must be aware of all such issues and consider their various dimensions and applicability in different markets where different certification bodies have jurisdiction.

Bibliography

Blech, Z.Y. (2008) *Kosher Food Production.* Ames, IA: Wiley-Blackwell.

Fischer, J. (2015b), Keeping enzymes kosher: Sacred and secular biotech production. EMBO Reports.

Lever, J. and Fischer, J. (2018) *Religion, Regulation, Consumption: Globalising Kosher and Halal Markets.* Manchester: Manchester University Press.

Riaz, M. N. and Chaudry, M. M. (2004) *Halal Food Production.* Boca Raton, FL: CRC Press.

11 Dairy production

Dairy is one of the oldest food industries and dairy products have been processed for human consumption for more than 5000 years. While kosher and halal requirements for producing dairy are very similar, halal requirements are not generally as strict, though in some instances dairy products can be considered kosher and halal at the same time (Riaz and Chaudry 2004). As we observed in the previous chapter, change is now occurring in both markets as biotechnology presents new opportunities to overcome many long-held concerns about contamination from animal-based ingredients.

Kosher

Kosher foods are either meat, dairy or parve (neither meat nor dairy) and Jewish dietary laws forbid the mixing of meat and milk. All foods derived from milk or containing milk are classed as dairy, including milk, butter, yoghourt and cheese. It goes without saying that all dairy kosher products must come from acceptable kosher animals and that all ingredients have to be free of animal derivatives, including rennet and gelatine, for example. Kosher dairy products must also be produced, processed and packaged in an appropriate way.

Antibiotics given to cows raise concerns about the status of milk, as do other ingredients routinely added to dairy products, including vitamins. While milk from kosher animals is by definition kosher, concerns that kosher milk can be mixed with non-kosher milk often lead to supervision of the milking process by competent *kashrut* authorities. There are many other concerns. Skimmed milk, for example, often has vitamin A added to it to address concerns that arise with the reduction of fat, while emulsifiers such as polysorbates are also added to vitamin supplements to make them soluble in milk; the use of sodium caseinate (a protein produced from casein in skimmed milk) and lactose must also be considered. Dairy cream, when fresh, has the same *halachic* status as milk, although powered milk processing raises concerns, and the cleansing of machinery may be necessary (Blech 2008). Much like cheese, yoghurt production can also pose problems, and all added ingredients must be kosher certified.

As we observed in Chapter 10, with the advent of biotechnology things have started to change. For example, rennet for cheese production was traditionally produced in calf stomachs, but today microbial alternatives can be produced artificially using biotechnology in large-scale industrial facilities. As companies are no longer dependent on particular animal species raised and slaughtered in specific ways, this has created the chance for businesses to do things differently in new locations, as we observe in more detail in the case of halal below.

Halal

The issues raised in halal dairy production are similar to those in kosher dairy production. Many dairy products are manufactured using haram and questionable ingredients added to milk and other dairy products, including vitamins and polysorbates, for example. There are also concerns about the enzymes used in cheese processing, which are often derived from pigs and animals that have been slaughtered inappropriately. Riaz and Chaudry (2004) provide an in-depth account of halal control points for a wide range of dairy products.

As well as the problems dairy creates for halal production, our work with a Malaysian company illustrates the business opportunities that are starting to emerge as a result of the development of new biotech solutions. The company in question wanted to produce an Italian cheese and certify it halal. The original Italian recipe stated that the cheese must be produced traditionally using calf rennet, which restricted production in Malaysia. With the advent of biotech production, however, the company realised they could manufacture the cheese in a country where rennet could be produced artificially in a laboratory. The company subsequently moved production to Eastern Europe from Malaysia, and they now market the product as an original Italian hard cheese, produced in Europe, certified by the HFCE (Lever and Fischer 2018).

Conclusion

There are many concerns in both kosher and halal dairy production about the threat of contamination from unacceptable ingredients. However, as we observed in this and the previous chapter, biotech production is creating new opportunities for businesses thinking about entering global kosher and halal markets. Moreover, these developments are creating new scientific standards for production, preparation, handling, storage and certification of kosher and halal products. Businesses entering these markets must be aware of these developments, not only because they are contested, but because they are also moving forward very quickly.

Bibliography

Blech, Z.Y. (2008) *Kosher Food Production*. Ames, IA: Wiley-Blackwell.

Lever, J. and Fischer, J. (2018) *Religion, Regulation, Consumption: Globalising Kosher and Halal Markets*. Manchester: Manchester University Press.

Riaz, M. N. and Chaudry, M. M. (2004) *Halal Food Production*. Boca Raton, FL: CRC Press.

12 Bread and the baking industry

Much like dairy, bread has long been a central aspect of the human diet. Mixing flour with water is the simplest way to make bread, but as with other food producers, commercial bakers add ingredients to bread and other baked products that present various concerns for kosher and halal production.

Kosher

Kosher bakeries and delicatessens are central features of Jewish communities around the world, and our research suggests that alongside meat, bread has a high kosher status, especially at Passover (Lever and Fischer 2018). There are some important kosher rules about bread to note at the outset. First, all 'standard' bread consumed with a meal must be Parve, thus ensuring that meat and dairy are not eaten together inadvertently. As white bread often contains dairy ingredients, this creates problems in modern production. There are some exceptions to this rule. Bread produced in unusual shapes, for example, or in small batches is not classed as 'standard' and is therefore exempt from this rule, as are cakes and biscuits. Second, historically there is a preference for kosher bread to be baked by Jews, which is still maintained to varying degrees by different certification bodies, notably at Passover (Blech 2008).

'Standard' kosher bread must be manufactured from dough that is mixed with water. Historically, dough was allowed to ferment naturally, and small amounts of fermented dough were used to leaven individual consignments of bread as and when required. Today, however, most of the bread produced in large bakeries uses commercial forms of yeast, which present particular concerns (Blech 2008); for example, many dough straighteners and conditioners contain enzymes derived from animal sources. Many large commercial bakeries also produce frozen or oven ready products for supermarkets, which also use enzymes to extend shelf life. This is a complex process, and while a dough producer may be kosher certified at the site of production, the end product sold at a supermarket may not be, unless of course the supermarket also has certification (Blech 2008). Many modern types of bread also contain oil or fats, which may be of animal origin; bread may also be processed using equipment that is used to produce bread containing animal ingredients, which again raises concerns.

As with other food products, kosher bread certification and/or bakery supervision thus revolves directly around the use of appropriate ingredients and equipment. The Orthodox Union (2008) explains:

> One of the challenges in certifying baked goods is the number of ingredients the average commercial bakery uses. It is not unusual for a bakery to use 500 ingredients; and many store over 1,000. Ingredients that need to be carefully monitored include oils, shortenings, flavors, emulsifiers, stabilizers, enzymes, glycerin, gelatin, grape juice, whey, and cheese.
>
> (Orthodox Union 2008)

Halal

As with kosher, halal bread and bakery certifications involve careful analysis of the ingredients and processes used during production to ensure compliance. Ingredients derived from animal sources present particular problems in commercial production, with oils and fats used to grease pans before baking being a particular concern. Many other questionable ingredients must be avoided in halal bread production, including food additives and flavourings (Riaz and Chaudry 2004). As much commercial bread contains these ingredients, it can be particularly difficult to find halal bread. During our research in Manchester, we came across a specialist halal bakery, Halal Mosam Bakery, which was set up to overcome these concerns. The owner explained that to overcome the issues involved, she only bakes bread and cakes made from vegetarian ingredients (Lever and Fischer 2018).

Case Study: Kingsmill bread

Halal bread presents significant business opportunities. The example of Kingsmill bread from Allied Bakeries (Associated British Foods Plc) provides a key example. In 2011 during a packaging relaunch, Kingsmill announced it had achieved certification from the UK's largest halal certification body, the Halal Food Authority (www.halalfoodauthority.eu). Many of the brand's products were already vegetarian and therefore suitable for a halal diet, but certification gave the brand greater recognition and status amongst halal consumers. As similar brands in the sector struggled, Kingsmill's willingness to target Muslim consumers while maintaining its traditional British identity helped to stabilise its market position. While their closest UK competitor, Hovis, experienced a US$112.1 million drop in sales in 2012–2013, Kingsmill remained dominant and in 2014 held down a 15.9% market share (Rownam 2015). More recently, the Sephardi Kashrut Authority in London (https://sephardikashrut.org.uk) has been working closely with Allied Bakeries to ensure that Kingsmill and other Allied Bakeries–branded products are kosher certified.

Conclusion

As staples of the human diet, bread and bakery products present particular problems and opportunities for kosher and halal production. Halal in particular is now a key growth area in packaged food in many Western countries, and businesses working in this sector need to be aware of the challenges involved if they are to make the most of these emerging opportunities.

Bibliography

Blech, Z.Y. (2008) *Kosher Food Production.* Ames, IA: Wiley-Blackwell.
Lever, J. and Fischer, J. (2018) *Religion, Regulation, Consumption: Globalising Kosher and Halal Markets.* Manchester: Manchester University Press.
Orthodox Union (2018) *Sweet-Talk: Inside The Kosher Bakery: From Exodus to the Modern Bakery*, https://oukosher.org/contact-us/, accessed 30 March 2018
Riaz, M. N. and Chaudry, M. M. (2004) *Halal Food Production.* Boca Raton, FL: CRC Press.
Rownam, A. (2015) Halal: A key growth area in British packaged food, *Doing Business in the Halal Market: Products, Trends and Growth Opportunities.* London: Euromonitor International, London.

13 Fruit and vegetables

When it comes to fruit and vegetables, kosher laws and regulation are somewhat stricter than halal. While all fruit and vegetables are classed as halal, fruit and vegetables can only be kosher if there is no contamination from insects.

Kosher

Kosher foods can be either meat, dairy or parve, that is neither meat nor dairy. In comparison to meat and meat products derived from the animal world, fruit and vegetables from the plant kingdom present lesser kosher concerns, unless of course they are processed or produced in ways that compromise kosher principles through the use of contaminated machinery or non-kosher additives (Blech 2008).

The most prominent kosher concern in this area relates to insect infestation, though it should be noted that some forms of locust are permissible. Insects are becoming popular as an alternative source of protein in the Western diet, yet they present a high risk from a kosher perspective, and controlling levels of infestation during food production is of the utmost importance. While it is recognised that there is no way of guaranteeing that all insects have been completely removed, concern about infestation is much higher than it is in the conventional food system, and it is therefore a central aspect of the kosher certification process. While a product may be certified vegetarian, this does not necessarily mean that it is kosher, and the threat of infestation must be considered in terms of the production region *and* the methods of production in use.

We encountered some of the issues involved during our research (Lever and Fischer 2018). Kellogg's production plant in Manchester is Europe's largest cereal factory with an output of approximately 400 million boxes of cereal a year. Kellogg's first started thinking about kosher certification in the late 1970s. At the time, they were spending 2 to 3 hours every month producing cereal for Israel. This meant that they had to close down production completely at great expense to comply with kosher requirements, and a decision was eventually made to get the factory fully kosher certified rather than continue with time-specific periods of supervision. All the cereal produced at the factory is now certified by Manchester Beth Din (MBD), which equates to a third of the one hundred Kellogg's cereal products currently manufactured in the UK. While many of the cereals produced at the factory are certified vegetarian, a rabbi conducting inspections explained this this does not mean that they are necessarily fully kosher. While the chocolate coatings on raisins have to be inspected to ensure that no animal derivatives the production of Fruit 'N' Fibre, for example, the rabbi pointed out that the raisins and sultanas in the mix also have to be inspected in great detail to ensure there is no insect infestation.

When it comes to vegetables, some are considered to be at a much greater than others. Broccoli, for instance, is seen to be particularly vulnerable, and it has therefore been banned from use in food production by some *kashrut* authorities; at the same time, some vegetables may also be unfit in one region and acceptable in another. Israeli produce presents more specific problems because of complex rules and restrictions about the ways in which fruit and vegetables are grown and harvested (see Blech 2008). There are also specific considerations over wine and grape juice from a kosher perspective (Blech 2008). Wine has a unique status in Jewish law, and there are restrictions on the production and handling of wine; all products containing wine or grape juice must remain in Jewish hands throughout the production process.

Case Study: UK producer of vegetarian products

During the course of our research, we spoke with a UK producer of meat-free, vegetarian products for kosher and halal markets around the world. Many of the company's customers are fast food chains. They supply kosher apple pies for McDonalds Israel halal apple pies and pie fillings for Macdonald's and Burger King in various locations, including the Middle East, South Africa, Egypt, Turkey and the UK. They also provide own-brand kosher and halal products in these markets.

The company has been working with McDonalds Israel for many and a rabbi must be on site at all times to supervise staff during production; the company has to plan ahead to accommodate the needs and requirements of the rabbi. The rabbi usually stays for a few days and will initially assess the production processes at the plant before giving the go-ahead to start production for a single batch of products that will be kosher approved. The rabbi's interpretation of what constitutes a kosher product is final, and building a good relationship with the rabbi is of the utmost importance for the company.

The company has also been producing products for the halal market for a number of years, particularly for countries in the Middle East. Our contact suggested that in recent years halal standards have become much more demanding. Until recently, there were (and still are) various differences between the halal authorities the company has to work with in different markets, but in the Middle East this has become much more straightforward in line with the emergence of stricter halal certification authorities in the region. The company has also recently started supplying halal products for Indonesia, which are certified by Indonesian Ulema Council (Majelis Ulama Indonesia – MUI), who were also said to set halal requirements at a very high level. As the company was already certified by the MUI-accredited Halal Food Authority (HFA) in the UK, this was a straightforward process.

Our contact suggested that the ways of working required in kosher and halal markets have been beneficial for the company and that they provide good safeguards against fraud that help to assure food safety: 'Whatever the product, if we're segregating it properly and we're only putting in the product the ingredients that should be in there, there's no cross-contamination.' The business opportunities on offer in kosher and halal markets were also seen to be high if the requirements of the relevant authorities and certification bodies are applied and adhered to in the correct way: 'It's no different to veganism or vegetarianism, and . . . there's an opportunity here that we can be trusted with . . . and we know they're going to come back to us every time because of the products we produce.' The implication here is that once a company gets over the fact that they may be working with religious criteria, the procedures involved actually enhance what the business is already doing, which presents 'an enormous business opportunity with such a large percentage of the world being Muslim'.

Halal

In general, insects have been condemned by Islamic scholars as *haram*, though as with kosher some forms of locust are acceptable. However, concerns about fruit and vegetables are not generally as strict for halal as they are for kosher. Most fresh fruits and vegetables are taken to be halal at face value, though of course they must always be washed thoroughly to get rid of any hidden contaminants.

Processed fruits and vegetable products present different types of problems, and they may be unacceptable if they are produced in factories that use non-halal ingredients such as fats, flavourings, preservatives and colourings during the production process (Riaz and Chaudry 2004).While many of the procedures used in this area do not require on-site supervision, a strong relationship with halal supervisory bodies is recommended to assure that nothing has compromised the halal status of the fruit and vegetables being used. Riaz and Chaudry (2004) also draw attention to the importance of labelling and packaging on fresh or frozen fruit products and to the fact that gelatine from unacceptable animals is often found in fruit juices.

Conclusion

In general, the requirements for fruit and vegetables are not as stringent as they are for meat and products, but kosher is somewhat stricter than halal. Although not generally seen as a key sector in the markets for kosher and halal food products, fruit and vegetables do however present significant business opportunities if companies working in this area adhere to the principles involved appropriately.

Bibliography

Blech, Z.Y. (2008) *Kosher Food Production*. Ames, IA:Wiley-Blackwell.
Lever, J. and Fischer, J. (2018) *Religion, Regulation, Consumption: Globalising Kosher and Halal Markets*. Manchester: Manchester University Press.
Riaz, M. N. and Chaudry, M. M. (2004) *Halal Food Production*. Boca Raton, FL: CRC Press.

14 Shops

In recent decades, halal/kosher food production has been lifted out of its traditional religious base in local community butcher shops and delicatessens into mainstream super- and hypermarkets. This chapter examines kosher/halal in this context. We discuss how super- and hypermarkets can live up to increasing halal and kosher requirements, not only in terms of keeping kosher/halal versus non-kosher/halal products seperate, but also the way in which – in some locations – shops are designed according to kosher/halal requirements. We also explore some of the controversies and opportunities involved.

Kosher

More than 80% of kosher food sold in the US is certified by the Big Five. While these agencies certify manufacturers, production and processing facilities, as well as products and product ingredients, their visibility and pre-eminence, particularly that of the OU, is even more evident in hyper- and supermarkets. In New York, Los Angeles, and many other locations across the US, up to two thirds of all kosher-certified products carry OU certification (Lytton 2013).

In recent decades food manufacturers in a number of European countries have also displayed a growing interest in kosher certification. In the UK and France, for example, there has been an increase in kosher labels and logos evident in mainstream supermarkets (Lever and Puig 2010). In areas of the UK with a high Jewish population, corporate retail chains such as Tesco and Sainsbury's now have separate kosher sections or sell kosher products. During the course of our research, we found a wide range of pre-packed kosher items in a number of super- and hypermarkets in Manchester. In specially designated world food areas, these stores have vertical freezers and chilled cabinets filled with kosher-branded meat, dairy and parve (neither meat nor dairy) products under the supervision of rabbinical authorities and certification bodies such as the London Beth Din (www. kosher.org.uk) and the Grand Rabbinate of Paris (www.consistoire.org).

Unlike the case of halal, it is not possible to buy fresh kosher meat in these shops. Kosher is more standardised than halal, and hyper- and supermarkets can only sell pre-packed kosher meat products that have been produced and processed elsewhere under the control of particular rabbinical authorities, often under supervision at market intermediaries such as Gilbert's Kosher Foods (www.gilbertskosherfoods.co.uk) in the UK; this company recently started supplying pre-packaged meat products with both kosher and halal certification. In the US, however, things can be different, and supermarkets often acquire certification to produce their own kosher-certified products – bread and bakery products, for example – in store (Blech 2008).

Our research suggests that the number of kosher butchers has declined some places in recent decades. While this could be related to the increasing presence of kosher labels and products in super- and hypermarkets, in cities with large Jewish populations there are now also high-class kosher supermarkets. Halpern's Kosher Food Store in Manchester is one such example. To some extent, the appearance of kosher-certified products in corporate retailers illustrates the move towards increasingly standardised ways of shopping, which is perhaps more evident in the case of halal.

Halal

As halal proliferated in urban Malaysia and Singapore in the 1980s, new shopping spaces and zones emerged to lift halal out of its traditional base in butcher shops into standardised super- and hypermarket contexts (Fischer 2011). A similar satiation emerged in Western countries in the first decades of the 21st century, when corporate retailers and market intermediaries became increasingly involved in the halal market.

Hypermarkets in Malaysia follow increasingly tight halal regulations and requirements, not only in terms of keeping halal and non-halal products separate, but also in relation to how more and more of these shops are designed according to particular halal requirements. *Tidak halal* (non-halal) products containing pork are either stored in a small, secluded room or on a specific counter away from the main shopping area in super/ hypermarkets, while wine and other alcoholic drinks are often stored in another room. Halal logos are ever present in this context, and they signify the transition away from personal, localised ways of shopping towards impersonal, regulated and standardised shopping characterised by changing relationships between seller, certifier and buyer.

Similar developments emerged in a number of European contexts in the first decades of the 21st century (Lever and Miele 2012). As opposed to Malaysia, however, some differences and complexities have emerged as a result of the competing halal requirements evident in this context. The most obvious difference in the UK is that it is halal products rather than non-halal products that are kept separate from the majority of super/ hypermarket product ranges, though perhaps the degree of separation is not as strong as it is in Malaysia. In the case of halal meat in particular, these developments have been made more complex and controversial by the availability of halal meat from both pre-stunned and non-stunned animals. While halal food is a booming sector in the UK, the case study that follows illustrates that it is also controversial, and that the placement of halal logos can be politically sensitive (Fernandez 2015).

Case Study: the halal meat controversy in the UK

The UK retailers ASDA and Tesco first started selling halal meat from pre-stunned animals certified by the HFA (www.halal foodauthority.eu) in 2000 and from 2007 and 2010 they both started selling meat from non-stunned animals (Lever and Miele 2012). Fresh non-stunned halal meat certified by the HMC (https://halal hmc.org) in partnership with the halal branding agency National Halal (http://nationalhalal.com) soon became visible on fresh halal meat counters in supermarkets in areas of the UK with a high Muslim population.

In subsequent years, as the availability of halal meat increased and controversy over slaughter methods and animal welfare grew, halal meat from pre-stunned animals became harder to identify. As a response to political controversy, certification bodies and their partners responded by hiding or being discreet about the placing of logos and certification marks on products and in-store (Fernadez 2015). Today, there are a wide range of own label supermarkets brands and value-added halal products produced by companies such as Haji Baba (www.hbhonline.co.uk) and Shazans (www.

shazans.com), for which it is hard to work out who provides certification and what the method of slaughter is. These developments are a direct result of political controversy about the production, provision and availability of halal meat in many Western countries (Lever and Fischer 2018).

Conclusion

This chapter has illustrated the different ways in which kosher, and perhaps to a greater extent halal, have become standardised and also politicised in different national and regional contexts through corporate food retailing. Although this often occurs for different reasons, businesses need to be aware of the issues involved when thinking about entering kosher and halal markets in different national and regional contexts.

Bibliography

Blech, Z.Y. (2008) *Kosher Food Production.* Ames, IA: Wiley-Blackwell.

Fernandez, R. (2015) Demand for halal food rising in tandem with growth of Southeast Asia, *Doing Business in the Halal Market: Products, Trends and Growth Opportunities.* London: Euromonitor International.

Fischer, J. (2011) *The Halal Frontier: Muslim Consumers in a Globalized Market.* New York: Palgrave Macmillan.

Lever, J. and Fischer, J. (2018) *Religion, Regulation, Consumption: Globalising Kosher and Halal Markets.* Manchester: Manchester University Press.

Lever J. and Miele, M. (2012) The growth of Halal meat markets in Europe: An exploration of the supply side theory of religion, *Journal of Rural Studies*, 28 (4), pp. 528–537.

Lever, J. and Puig, M. (2010) The development of Halal and Kosher meat markets in the UK, *Dialrel Factsheet*, www.dialrel.eu/images/factsheet-market-uk.pdf

Lytton, T. D. (2013) *Kosher Private Regulation in the Age of Industrial Food.* Cambridge: Harvard University Press.

Riaz, M. N. and Chaudry, M. M. (2004) *Halal Food Production.* Boca Raton, FL: CRC Press.

15 Restaurants

In this chapter, we explore kosher/halal in local restaurants as well as in global chains such as McDonald's. Many of the trends we saw in the previous chapter are evident in this sector.

Kosher

Kosher restaurants and delicatessens have long been a central element of Jewish neighbourhoods around the world. But today it is not just Jewish consumers who purchase kosher. A recent study found that more than 60% of kosher food consumption in the US is linked to non-religious values associated with health and food quality (Mintel 2009). In recent decades, kosher food has also become associated with ethnic cuisine (Lever and Puig 2010), including Asian and Mexican food, for example, and certification bodies now offer certification for a growing range of restaurants. Different cuisines present different problems from a kosher perspective, although the primary factor in the kosher status of a restaurant primarily revolves around its 'dairy' or 'meat' standing (Blech 2008).

    The levels of *kashrut* supervision needed in a restaurant are also much more intensive than they are in a meat factory or food manufacturing company. While the high volumes of raw materials and ingredients used in a factory can be inspected through regular checks of records and unannounced spot checks/visits, in a restaurant it is much more difficult to ensure and safeguard all the complex elements of production. For example, restaurants buy ingredients in smaller quantities from numerous vendors. The source of ingredients may change at short notice due to supply-side problems, while brokers may also be involved in the supply chain. Fresh vegetables can be problematic because of insect infestation; fresh eggs must be individually inspected; and segregation must be maintained between meat and fish. To address these and other related concerns, a kosher supervisor or suitably qualified kosher manager is required in a restaurant at all times to enable each aspect of production to be controlled and kosher status and integrity maintained; dairy-only restaurants are less complex (Blech 2008).

Because of the complexities involved, fast food restaurants specialising in a high turnover of cheap products for the mass market are not frequently kosher certified. While McDonald's and Burger King have outlets in Israel, not all are kosher certified. There are also kosher fast food restaurants, Subway for example, in New York City and other locations in the US, though perhaps not as many as there once were. Our research shows that in other cities with large Jewish populations, in London and Manchester in the UK, for example, there are also many locally certified high-class kosher restaurants. In these locations, it is also possible to find smaller kosher-certified Indian and Chinese restaurants/takeaways and smaller independent fast food restaurants, where the cost of certification and supervision are not so prohibitive (Lever and Fischer 2018).

Halal

Similar developments are evident in the global halal market. In Malaysia and Singapore local restaurants as well as global chains such as McDonald's are subject to increasing halal requirements. Many of the trends we saw observed in the previous chapter are evident in this context too, in Europe as well as in South East Asia and the Middle East.

Much like hyper- and supermarkets, since the 1980s restaurants in Singapore and Malaysia have had to deal with and address rising halal requirements. In the early 1980s, the Singaporean certifier MUIS announced that Muslims should not eat meat at restaurants without halal certificates after concerns were expressed by Kentucky Fried Chicken (KFC) about pork in burgers; when McDonalds subsequently opened in Malaysia it was difficult to get halal meat that was acceptable to MUIS. As more fast food restaurants became halal certified, they came under increasing pressure to assure the public that what they served fully complied with Islamic regulations, and the appropriate display of halal signs and logos became a critical issue (Fischer 2015a).

For outlets to be certified halal, everything – from the ingredients used in production to food preparation and customer service – now has to conform to Islamic standards. In order to obtain halal status, MUIS also requires that restaurants hire at least two Muslim staff at each outlet to ensure that all regulations are complied with. After McDonald's was halal certified by MUIS in the early 1990s, animal slaughter, food preparation, and cleaning had to be carried out by Muslims. Two Muslims had to be employed in each restaurant to verify the halal status of the food, and restaurants had to give MUIS access at all times to carry out spot checks and ensure that halal standards were adhered to.

In 1995 fast food restaurants in Malaysia were halal certified by the Malaysian certifier JAKIM for the first time. In both Malaysia and Singapore, fast food chains such as McDonald's and KFC are now subject to rigorous inspections to ensure ritual cleanliness and guarantee their restaurants are fit to be halal certified. Restaurant owners become halal certified to expand their customer base among the local Muslim population, and they have to make the choice of finding a satisfactory way of working with unlawful (haram) foods or eliminate them altogether. In this context, halal logos and certificates play a major role in restaurants selling standardised halal products (Fischer 2015a). UK food businesses working with fast food chains such as MacDonald's and Burger King in Muslim countries suggested that as UAE standards become increasingly important in the global market, the processes involved are becoming stricter but also more straightforward.

Similar developments have emerged in a number of Western countries in the 21st century. In 2009, the HFA in the UK went into partnership with KFC to supply certified halal meat from stunned animals in more than 100 restaurants in areas of the UK with a high Muslim population. This was primarily in London, although the scheme was eventually extended more widely. Many other UK fast food and restaurant chains now sell halal-certified meat and poultry, including Nando's, Subway, Domino's Pizza and Pizza Express. As in the case of super- and hypermarkets in the UK, these developments have been made more complex by the politicised distinction between halal meat from pre-stunned and non-stunned animals, and it is often difficult to find information about certification partners and methods of slaughter on the menus of these restaurants, which has been controversial for the business involved (Lever and Fischer 2018).

The complexity involved was evident at an Italian restaurant in central Manchester during the course of our research (Lever and Fischer 2018). Although the restaurant is not halal certified, the manager has a certificate from a supplier of non-stunned meat certified by the HMC that he shows to customers when they ask if the restaurant's meat is halal. Although customers never ask if the restaurant's meat is from stunned or non-stunned animals, viewing this certificate satisfies their curiosity, and once they have seen the certificate the manger suggested that they rarely ask to see it on subsequent visits. As in the kosher market, our research highlights an increasing number of different ethnic restaurants providing halal in cities such as Manchester, including Brazilian, Turkish, Spanish and Italian.

Conclusion

This chapter has illustrated both the opportunities and the problems restaurants encounter when they enter kosher and halal markets. In the kosher market in particular, costs can be prohibitive, such are the complexities involved. With halal, the appropriate display of halal logos is an issue of concern both in South-East Asia and in Western countries, but for different reasons. As we have stated previously, the issues faced by businesses thinking about entering kosher and halal markets are context specific, and restaurants must always remember this important point.

Bibliography

Blech, Z.Y. (2008) *Kosher Food Production.* Ames, IA: Wiley-Blackwell.
Fischer, J. (2015a) *Islam, Standards and Technoscience: In Global Halal Zones.* London and New York: Routledge.
Lever, J. and Fischer, J. (2018) *Religion, Regulation, Consumption: Globalising Kosher and Halal Markets.* Manchester: Manchester University Press.
Lever, J. and Puig, M. (2010) The development of Halal and Kosher meat markets in the UK, *Dialrel Factsheet*, www.dialrel.eu/images/factsheet-market-uk.pdf
Mintel (2009) *Kosher Foods – US –* January 2009. Mintel.

16 The food service industry and public institutions

Introduction

Outside worship some of the earliest activities of Jewish and Muslim migrants centred on the provision of kosher and halal food in local eateries, and later on in the demand for kosher and halal food in public institutions (Lever and Fischer 2018). Following on from previous chapters on shops (Chapter 14) and restaurants (Chapter 15), in this chapter we focus on the provision of kosher and halal food in public institutions (schools, hospitals and airlines).

Schools and hospitals

Kosher and halal food is available in public institutions in many Western countries. For example, in areas of the UK with a high Jewish or Muslim population our research suggests that many mainstream schools and hospitals provide kosher and halal meals alongside other specialist dietary requirements (Lever and Fischer 2018). In Kirklees in West Yorkshire, for example, which has a large South Asian population, all school menus provided by the local authority catering team are planned in line with the Government's School Food Standards, which aim to provide appropriate meals for *all* children, including halal (Kirklees 2015). There are similar arrangements in other countries (Giorda, Bossi and Messina 2014). However, some schools in the UK are not large enough to provide different types of food for every cultural group, and some therefore provide meat that can be eaten by Muslims and non-Muslims alike; as with the provision of halal meat in supermarkets and restaurants, this can be a source of controversy (Lever and Fischer 2018).

Alongside their large Muslim population, Manchester and Salford in the UK also have a large Jewish population. Kosher food and snacks are therefore available in public institutions such as schools and hospitals across the region, very often alongside halal food options. National Health Service (NHS) food standards in the UK also cover halal and kosher food (NHS 2016). Our research found that while kosher and halal food options are available as standard in many NHS hospitals, some hospitals and schools also provide pre-packed meals from companies such as Hermolis (www. hermolis.com). This company, which also provides pre-packed kosher and halal meals for British Airways (see below), is certified by a variety of certification bodies in different locations.

Airlines

An increasing number of airlines and airports provide kosher and halal food for passengers and travellers. The airline industry is by definition multicultural, flying tourists and business people around the globe from one destination to another. Food is an integral part of the overall in-flight experience, and in-flight services play an important role in customer satisfaction. If they are not provided as standard, many airlines will order a pre-packaged kosher or halal meal for passengers on request. There are many other related services provided at airports.

As the kosher market has grown, the demand for kosher food and associated services has expanded rapidly, and it is now possible to find hotels that are either fully kosher certified or under kosher supervision. The demand for kosher airline meals has also been growing for some time, and there is now an increasing demand for *glatt* meals as well as standard kosher meals (Kosher Today 2013). In North America, Gate Gourmet (www.gategourmet.com) – one of the world's leading airline catering companies – provides kosher food for a number of airlines. They have kosher-supervised kitchens at Trudeau Airport in Montreal and at Pearson International Airport in Toronto. In the United States eight major airlines, including American and Continental, sell OU-certified kosher food on board.

In Europe, there are numerous caterers providing similar services. The Dutch company Langerhuize (www.langerhuize.nl) provides kosher meals for many global airlines, including KLM, Air France and Alitalia, as well as for caterers such as Gate Gourmet. In the UK, Hermolis provides a similar service to more than sixty airlines, including British Airways. Many caterers serving airlines around the world are supervised by local rabbinate or certification agencies. In the UK, Hermolis is certified by Kedassia and the Kashrut Division of the London Beth Din (www.klbdkosher.org). The company also provides halal airline meals certified by Halal Consultations (http://halalconsultations.com).

As well as serving the kosher market, Gate Gourmet also offers halal meals (see case study below). Another large global caterer serving the airline industry, LSG Group (www.lsgskychefs.com) has also set up halal production facilities. Certified by relevant local partners at airports around the world, these range from small and medium-small facilities all the way up to large-scale kitchens producing thousands of halal meals a day. The certification process involves:

- Halal ingredients
- Detailed audits of kitchen areas
- Detailed audits of suppliers
- Comprehensive training
- Consultation services

Case Study: Japan airlines and airports

In recent years, the increasing demand for halal food by travellers and business people has been recognised in Japan. Narita Airport and Kansia Airports have opened restaurants serving halal food from Gate Gourmet certified by Malaysian certification bodies. Other businesses linked to the Japanese tourist industry have also moved in this direction, offering Muslim travellers halal-certified Japanese food options to enhance the tourist experience. Until recently, Japan Airlines (JAL) only served halal meals to Muslim passengers on request as a special option. However, when JAL acquired halal certification from the Japan Islamic Trust (www.islam.or.jp) in 2016 for production methods as well as for product ingredients, they began to offer halal-certified meals on all international flights out of Japan. The Japan Islamic Trust is approved by halal-certifying agencies in the United Arab Emirates, Qatar and Thailand, giving it global coverage. Such meals are now also available on flights from Jakarta, Indonesia and Malaysia into Japan; all are served on disposable dishware to assure Muslim customers. Some JAL meals are also specially blessed and sealed in line with the kosher requirements of Jewish passengers.

As well as their availability of flights, kosher and halal products are increasingly visible and available to airline passengers at terminals around the world. Heathrow Airport's retail portal in the UK now lists kosher and halal options around its terminals alongside other special dietary products.

Conclusion

Kosher and halal food is now widely available in public institutions around the world. As in other sectors, certification plays a central role in this context. To make the most of the business opportunities these developments offer, companies wishing to work in this environment must consider kosher and halal food options alongside other special dietary requirements if they are to meet the needs of all their customers.

Bibliography

Giorda, M., C., Bossi, L. and Messina, E. (2014) *Food and Religion (in public food service)*, www.eurel.info/IMG/pdf/report_2014_food_and_religion_in_public_food_service_.pdf

Kirklees Council (2015) *Schools and Education*, www.kirklees.gov.uk/beta/schools/primary-and-middle-school-meals.aspx

Kosher Today (2013) *Airlines Increasingly Cater to Kosher Travelers Worldwide*, www.koshertoday.com/airlines-increasingly-cater-to-kosher-travelers-worldwide/

Lever, J. and Fischer, J. (2018) *Religion, Regulation, Consumption: Globalising Kosher and Halal Markets. Manchester:* Manchester University Press.

NHS (2016) *Hospital Services: Hospital Food Standards*, https://www.nhs.uk/NHS England/AboutNHSservices/NHShospitals/Pages/hospital-food-standards.aspx

17 Training

This chapter discusses the importance of kosher/halal training offered by kosher/halal businesses and certifiers. Training is not only important for generating knowledge of kosher/halal in businesses, it is also an opportunity for networking between businesses and certifiers. In a way, training can be seen to 'standardise' kosher/halal understanding and practice between businesses and certifiers, thus creating shared assumptions about what proper kosher/halal production or trade are or should be. Training is also about enhancing kosher/halal skills in businesses with specific regard to communication, team building and leadership. In many cases employees will take training as a team that is responsible for kosher/halal in the business, thus creating opportunities for wider knowledge sharing and further training. Here we deal with two types of training.

Firstly, there is training arranged by a kosher/halal certifier for business staff participation. Some businesses may be hesitant to participate in such training because they find it unnecessary or costly. However, many businesses find that training provides them with knowledge they could not have acquired otherwise, and that in some cases trainers from certification bodies also act as inspectors/auditors. In this way training can be seen as a platform for establishing a more personal relationship between business and certifier. Secondly, there is training within businesses, and the bigger the business the more pertinent this kind of training will be. Many multinational companies have set up positions such as kosher/halal coordinators, and employees in these positions are often responsible for the training of other staff, both locally and globally.

Kosher/halal training courses are often advertised in e-mails, at kosher/halal network events and/or food fairs and described on relevant websites.

Training case study 1: Novozymes

Novozymes (discussed in Chapter 1) is the leading enzyme manufacturer globally. The company has enzyme plants in Denmark, the US, China, India, Brazil and Canada. Novozymes started undergoing auditing for Jewish dietary law (*kashrut*) compliance in the late 1980s and is certified by the leading kosher certifier Orthodox Union (OU), and to comply with divergent halal requirements set by Islamic organisations globally the company's products are certified by several halal certifiers. Novozymes trains all staff involved in kosher and halal production, and this case study focuses on a kosher/halal training that took place at the company's headquarters in Denmark in 2018. The researcher was invited to give a talk on kosher/halal trends, and this allowed for lively discussion and the opportunity to act as an observer during the training. A company such as Novozymes considers training essential for kosher/halal compliance and invests the necessary resources to bring together kosher/halal managers from around the world regularly.

During the two days of training the company's global halal and kosher coordinator focuses on updating new and old staff on kosher/halal, and he starts out with *Background & History* with reference to the latest developments surrounding kosher/halal products and their status types. Moving on to *Origin & Basic Rules*, the coordinator explains about the role of animal ingredients; mixtures with meat; ingredients and a number of additional issues related to the Jewish festival of Passover, which calls for specific rules. Then a session on *Certification Bodies* follows, which starts with an overview of all the kosher/halal certification bodies the company works with: there is a specific on the legal contract drawn up between the company and various certifiers and the relevant contact persons in kosher/halal bodies. The issue of which certifiers currently (mis)recognise other certifiers, especially regarding halal, also falls under this theme. With regard to *Ingredients & Materials* the discussion mostly focuses on main-ingredient rules against those ingredients/materials that requires approval – for example, with regard to OU approvals there are six different groups or types.

Contamination is a central issue in kosher and also to a lesser extent in halal. Moreover, kosher contamination is an issue that must be dealt with from two perspectives: firstly, in connection with production processes taking place when the temperature is above 46° and below 46° Celsius. Lastly, this topic deals with the '1% rule', that is, if the content of ingredients with lower kosher status is below 1% it will not contaminate products with higher kosher status. Secondly, there is the issue of kosherization discussed earlier. In terms of *Production*, the focus is mainly on kosher and targets facilities/equipment/processes, raw materials and the 1% rule in connection with fermentation. When we reach the theme *Laboratories* central issues are specific laboratory processes with special focus on kosher re-tapping of laboratory equipment. Lastly, the issue of *Logistics, Labelling & Toll Manufacturing* focuses on approval and supervision of facilities; approved Novozymes sites/manufacturers; toll manufacturers; relabelling at non-OU supervised warehouses; status after re-tapping; transfer of concentrates between sites; bulk transportation and storage; bulk transportation of Group 4 raw materials that warrant documentation to ensure that these have not been transported with anything non-kosher and Food Grade products; as well as receiving control of Group 4 raw materials. The two-day training consists of presentations by the coordinator, staff and invited speakers as well as exercises. Training such as this one focuses equally on kosher and halal, but because kosher is more complex in a number of respects it often occupies a more central role compared to halal. Conversely, the issue of certifiers that variously (mis)recognise other certifiers is more important in halal.

Training case study 2:   MUIS Academy in Singapore

This case concerns Halal Training at MUIS Academy in Singapore. This training consisted of two courses: *Level 1: Halal Foundation*

Programme with an Introduction to the Singapore MUIS Halal Quality Management System (HalalMQ) and *Level 2: Halal Training Programme. Developing & Implementing Halal Quality Management System (HalMQ).* The basic structure of the training is a series of slides. The trainer explains about the days programme that runs from 9am to 5pm and consists of lectures, team exercises, problem solving and case studies, as well as questions and answers. The course is mandatory, and it is aimed at halal team members, halal liaison officers, managers and supervisors from companies and state institutions who are responsible for halal certification, as well as Muslim employees.

QUIZ 1 is on *What is halal?* This question is discussed in groups for a while. QUIZ 2 is on *What Is Halal Certification?* Groups again discuss, and the accompanying slides to a large extent focus on MUIS's role in halal certification and its accompanying legislation. Before moving to Team Exercise 1: *What are your benefits to halal certification?*, the fees for the different number of MUIS halal certification schemes are outlined.

HalMQ implementation plans for new and existing halal certificate holders are discussed next, as well as ten detailed HalMQ principles, for example establishing the halal team. After a discussion of the application process, *Team Exercise 2* deals with the issues touched upon in groups. After group work, groups present their discussions and findings, and there is also room for queries: a woman asks how large the MUIS halal logo on products can be, and the trainer replies that this depends on the size of products, that is, there has to be fair relationship between the size of the logo and the product surface. Finally, the teacher issues certificates to participants.

The trainer who taught Level 1 is also responsible for Level 2, and the basic structure of the course is the same. The trainer starts out by explaining how this Level 2 course develops some of the points raised in Level 1 and leads to a Level 3 course on *Conducting Halal Internal Audits. Level 2: Developing and Implementing Halal Quality Management System (HalMQ)* starts with the basic structure of the course is *General Halal Certification Requirements; Introduction to HalMQ, 10 principles of HalMQ* and a *Maintenance Programme*, which overall focuses on the keys to maintaining a good halal system.

In *Group Exercise 1* participants must list the benefits of Implementing HalMQ. In *Exercise 2* participants have to imagine that they are halal team members and document the profile of the Team and the nature of products and business. In *Exercise 3* groups have to develop a flow chart for business operations and identify possible threats and control measures.

The second day of the course starts with a discussion of principles for the establishment of a monitoring system and corrective action for each halal access point (HAP) followed by an exercise on these topics. During a break the trainer explains that essentially halal is an Islamic injunction and that quite a number of questions about halal can only be answered by religious scholars. For example, for fish to be halal they must have scales, and imams determined this in a *fatwa* (opinion concerning Islamic law issued by an Islamic scholar). Another issue is that these interpretations and rulings differ between the different schools of Islamic jurisprudence. The trainer contends that halal is not an exact science, and but is open to interpretation and that MUIS plays a central role in this type of interpretation and regulation. After discussing principles on establishing documentation and record keeping, verifying the halal system and reviewing the halal system the trainer issues certificates to all participants, and this concludes the course.

Conclusion

Kosher/halal training plays an important role for businesses with regard to learning, but it also provides and enhances personal contact between businesses and certifiers. We know from our research that many certifiers also enjoy training as a more informal type of interaction with businesses. Many businesses already participate in other types of training arranged by state or local authorities, for example, and kosher/halal training is comparable to non-religious types of training. Hence, businesses can also consider how they can draw on existing experiences with other types of training to select the appropriate training programme in this context. They should therefore consider similar kinds of questions: What are the specific needs of the business? Are there certain issues that the business would like to bring up or negotiate during training? Could several businesses take the same training programme together to 'standardise' and share knowledge?

Most importantly, perhaps, training can generate a common managerial model that emphasises the encouragement of internal compliance systems. More specifically, training can help businesses comply with issues such as standards, production, preparation, handling and storage of kosher/halal ingredients and products.

Bibliography

Fischer, J. (2015) *Islam, Standards and Technoscience: In Global Halal Zones*. London and New York: Routledge.

18 Science

This chapter explores kosher and halal in the context of 'religious' science. Much like the science of food safety, kosher and halal production is concerned with preventing the adulteration of food. Given the complex web of global food production, it is no longer possible for kosher and halal consumers to ascertain the origin of many raw materials, so science plays an increasingly important role in interactions between religious regulations and secular production. Fifty years ago, an individual food product may have contained only five ingredients, but today a single food item may contain hundreds of ingredients sourced from many different locations. In this changing context, businesses whose products are accused of not living up to religious standards can be held to account, and more and more kosher and halal products are thus subjected to testing for unwanted ingredients by certification bodies and, in the case of halal in particular, by laboratories at religious universities.

Kosher and science

Chapter 10 demonstrated that science is increasingly important in the field of kosher biotech, yet science is also important in other areas of kosher production. Although most kosher practices are based on religious beliefs, in some cases it appears that they often have a practical basis in science.

We came across some of the issues involved during our research at Kellogg's in Manchester, where one of the largest cereal factories in the world is located (Lever and Fischer 2018). During an inspection, a rabbi from Manchester Beth Din examines a series of large machines in which ingredients for Kellogg's kosher certified products are sorted. In a huge hall, a number of large rotating cylindrical pressure cookers heat millions of corn grits using steam, a process that has the potential to create many problems for kosher production. In another part of the factory, where corn flakes are toasted, flavoured and tossed on conveyor belts, engineers are consulted to understand the implications of the heating process. As this example illustrates, the 'kosherness' of products is not easily verifiable.

A similar process was evident in a factory during the course of our research in Malaysia. When OU and OK rabbinic supervisors visit the factory for an inspection they perform a test that involves tasting water in a steam boiler that contains traces of non-kosher material to make sure that it has a bitter and unpleasant taste. The test involves a bitter substance such as Bitrex (the most bitter substance known) being added to the boiler to make the water unpalatable to humans and suitable for ritual cleaning. This type of test can only be done during an inspection, and it testifies to the significance of scientific practices that take place on these occasions.

Recognised scientific tests are also used in kosher production to detect the presence of unwanted ingredients. For example, a polymerase chain reaction analysis can be used to detect minute traces of porcine DNA, thus helping with the detection of non-kosher ingredients and products (Fischer 2015a). The globalisation of food production has given large kashrut organisations such as Orthodox Union (www.ou.org) and Organized Kashrut (www.ok.org) an increasingly important role in this arena; science is moving forward fast and new tests are appearing on the market. These developments are perhaps more evident in the halal industry, where there is a growing interest in the relationship between Islam and science (Iqbal 2012).

Halal science

The question of how halal fits into a whole range of modern Islamic scientific and secular processes is only just starting to be addressed. Those who advocate for the Islamisation of knowledge tend to argue that science is neutral and that it is the attitude by which we approach science that makes it secular or Islamic (Iqbal 2012).

In Malaysia, science is intricately linked to politics, state priorities and halal research agendas. Malaysia is a hub of scientific expertise, and there are a number of important institutions in the country, including the Islamic Science University of Malaysia (www.usim.edu.my). The World Halal Forum, the leading global halal network event globally, which is held in Malaysia, brings together Islamic organisations, halal certifiers, politicians, scientists and companies. This event testifies to Malaysia's leading global position as a laboratory for the setting of new standards for halal production, preparation, handling, storage, regulation and science. The state of Malaysia has effectively driven these halal standards since the 1980s, but it is only within the last decade or so that halal has been fully integrated with a localised form of Islamic science.

Scholars from the Institute of Halal Food at Universiti Putra Malaysia (www.upm.edu.my) found that food manufacturers often choose lard as a substitute ingredient for oil because it is cheaper and more readily available. In collaboration with Islamic Science University of Malaysia, these scholars thus developed a method for species identification by extracting the DNA of pork and lard from pork and lard samples, which they suggest is a reliable technique for detection of pig meat and fat.

Further research by the group on a method for the detection of the presence of pig derivatives extracted genomic DNA from sausages, bread and biscuits, thus providing a new method for the detection of pork adulteration and fraudulent species substitution in halal food production (Fischer 2015a). Through these developments, Islamic science and modern halal have become inseparable from the Malaysian state and the secular syllabuses required by the Ministry of Higher Education to attract external funding for halal research.

Malaysian scholars are also involved in attempts to remove alcohol from food production processes (Riaz and Chaudry 2004). However, halal food scientists from the HFCE claim that while it is possible to remove 97 to 98% of ethanol from flavourings, the energy and the effort required to complete this process is currently very high, thus making the cost of the goods involved prohibitively expensive for many Muslims. Nevertheless, as a result of these developments, the Malaysian Government recently signed a Memorandum of Understanding (MoU) with a UK science company for the establishment of halal proficiency testing. This agreement enables Fera Science (www.fera.co.uk) to pursue the development of protocols to detect low levels of pork and alcohol in halal products (Fuseini, Wotton, Knowles and Hadley 2017).

Many such issues, as indicated, are as much about politics as they are about science. During the course of our research we heard instances of global companies trying to export products to Germany encountering problems because the German halal certifier Halal Control (www.halal control.eu) has little tolerance for alcohol. Controversy over science is evident in other areas of production. For example, there is no overall scientific consensus about what constitutes the most 'humane' way of slaughtering animals for food: as well as being scientific, the issue is also ethical and subject to interpretation (Bergeaud-Blackler 2007). Businesses need to be aware of all such issues when entering kosher and halal markets in different regional contexts.

Conclusion

As we observed in Chapter 10, science is increasingly important in the field of kosher/halal biotech production, where the commercial ambition of many food companies has created a secondary market of kosher and halal auditing and certification. In this chapter, we have seen another dimension of these developments, which allows companies whose products do not live up to religious standards to be held to account through new scientific tests for unacceptable ingredients. We have also seen that many scienfic processes are often of a highly political and contested nature. Businesses entering these must be aware of all such issues.

Bibliography

Bergeaud-Blackler, F. (2007) New challenges for Islamic ritual slaughter: A European perspective, *Journal of Ethnic and Migration Studies*, 33 (6), pp. 965–980.

Fischer, J. (2015a) *Islam, Standards, and Technoscience: In Global Halal Zones*. London and New York: Routledge.

Fuseini, A., Wotton, S. B., Knowles, T. G. and Hadley, P. J. (2017) Halal meat Fraud and safety issues in the UK, *Food Ethics*. First Online: 26 January 2017.

Iqbal, M. (ed) (2012) *Islam and Science: Historic and Contemporary Perspectives*. Farnham: Ashgate.

Lever, J. and Fischer, J. (2018) *Religion, Regulation, Consumption: Globalising Kosher and Halal Markets*. Manchester: Manchester University Press.

Riaz, M. N. and Chaudry, M. M. (2004) *Halal Food Production*. Boca Raton, FL: CRC Press.

Part IV

Conclusions

19 Conclusions

We now tie the findings of the book together by considering a range of issues that are central to the proliferation of global markets for religiously certified products and their future development.

We have seen throughout the book how global markets for kosher and halal products – not only food but also biotech products and other ingredients – have increased in significance as kosher and halal have been lifted out of their traditional religious base in communities. While companies may encounter new challenges and greater complexities in these markets through increased inspections and audits, for example, and in demands for the greater traceability of ingredients, they may also encounter new opportunities and market niches where they can innovate and develop new product lines.

In Part I of the book we explored definitions of kosher and halal as well as their similarities and differences. A key point to note here is that many companies thinking about achieving halal certification already have kosher certification and that there are clear synergies between the two. In Part II of the book we looked at some of the key issues within kosher and halal markets in more depth, notably the role of certification, logos and standards, as well as limitations of government and the demands of consumers. Some important considerations worth repeating are that inspections and the appropriate display of kosher and halal logos are important aspects of everyday production, trade and consumption that allow branded messages to be communicated effectively. At the same time, however, it is worth noting some of the complexities involved. In South East Asia, for example, certification and the placement of halal logos are a central aspect of business engagement. In Western countries such as the UK, by way of contrast, political controversy around animal welfare and animal slaughter practice has created tensions over labelling and the placement of logos. While halal is a booming sector in this part of the world, it is also controversial.

In each national context or region businesses work in, they must comply with all relevant legislation as well as the certification requirements of relevant organisations. In the kosher market, this often means working with the Big Five, who many companies hold in high regard but who are also considered monopolistic and expensive by smaller certifiers. Similar conditions exist in the halal market, where the major certifiers recognise smaller certifiers on an on-and-off basis. In a complex and rapidly changing global context, it is therefore important that businesses consult the websites of major certifiers regularly to understand and keep abreast of developments in different regional contexts. Companies should also remember that certification bodies are, much like other businesses, looking to build relationships and that any difficult issues and challenges can be overcome through negotiation.

It is clear from the material presented in Part III of the book that the global markets for kosher and halal present significant business opportunities. Biotech products are one such example, and in an era of regular food scares and rising religious requirements, non-animal ingredients can be less problematic than ingredients derived from animal sources. The example of the Malaysian company relocating to Europe to produce a halal-certified Italian cheese discussed in Chapter 11 illustrates the scope of these opportunities. There is also untapped potential in areas not traditionally seen as important sectors for kosher and halal products, including fruit and vegetables. In Chapter 13 we discussed this potential through a case study of a UK company producing meat-free, vegetarian and parve products for fast food chains working in kosher and halal markets in different regional contexts. Moreover, as we observed in Chapter 18, as the links between religious certification and the scientific verification of products as kosher and halal expands, opportunities are emerging for companies providing scientific products.

Another important point to note in this conclusion is that developments in biotechnology are not only generating new business opportunities, they are also creating new scientific standards and new forms of knowledge. As Chapter 17 demonstrates, implementing training across a business is one way in which the issues involved – production, preparation, handling and storage of kosher/halal ingredients and products – can be standardised to allow business to achieve wider compliance and greater recognition.

Finally, it is worth remembering that kosher and halal consumers have varying demands and requirements in different global locations and regional contexts. In the US, for instance, which has a huge kosher market, there is growing recognition of the higher quality and health benefits associated with kosher food, while consumers in South East Asia and the Middle East are becoming more fastidious about halal. Understanding the changing requirements and benefits of religious production and certification allows businesses to engage in these markets in new and innovative ways, thus allowing them to engage with the growing number of consumers that see the benefits that religiously certified products offer.

Index

Printed in the United States
by Baker & Taylor Publisher Services